The Ultimate Super Easy Mediterranean Diet Cookbook

150 Quick, Delicious, and Fully Colored Recipes for Healthy Everyday Meals

SOPHIA HOLM

Copyright Notice

CONTENTS

INTRODUCTION

1. What is the Mediterranean Diet?

The Mediterranean Diet is a way of eating inspired by the traditional dietary patterns of countries bordering the Mediterranean Sea, such as Greece, Italy, Spain, and southern France. It emphasizes whole, fresh, and natural ingredients, celebrating the rich flavors and cultural heritage of the region. Recognized as one of the healthiest diets globally, it is both a culinary tradition and a lifestyle that promotes physical and mental well-being.

Origins and Cultural Significance

The Mediterranean Diet reflects the culinary traditions of the Mediterranean Basin, dating back thousands of years. This diet evolved from the practices of agricultural communities, where meals were prepared with locally available, seasonal ingredients. The cuisine is deeply rooted in cultural rituals, family gatherings, and the celebration of food as a communal experience.

Countries such as Greece, Italy, and Spain exemplify this diet, where olive oil, fresh vegetables, grains, and seafood take center stage. Staples like bread, wine, and cheese are often incorporated in moderation, reflecting a balanced approach to indulgence. The Mediterranean Diet is more than just a nutritional plan; it's a lifestyle that fosters mindfulness, social connections, and sustainability.

Health Benefits

The Mediterranean Diet is consistently ranked as one of the healthiest diets in the world, with a wide range of evidence-based health benefits:

1. **Heart Health:**
   - Rich in healthy fats, primarily from olive oil, nuts, and fish, the diet helps reduce bad cholesterol (LDL) and increase good cholesterol (HDL).
   - It lowers the risk of heart disease and stroke, thanks to its anti-inflammatory and cardiovascular-protective properties.

2. **Weight Management:**
   - The diet emphasizes nutrient-dense foods that are naturally low in calories and high in fiber, keeping you full and satisfied.
   - It encourages mindful eating, which supports sustainable weight loss and maintenance.

3. **Longevity:**
   - Studies show that populations adhering to this diet have lower rates of chronic diseases like diabetes, cancer, and Alzheimer's, contributing to increased life expectancy.
   - The diet's focus on antioxidants, from fruits, vegetables, and herbs, reduces oxidative stress and slows aging processes.

4. **Mental Health:**
   - The Mediterranean Diet has been linked to improved mood and reduced risks of depression, attributed to its balanced fats, whole grains, and nutrient-rich foods.

Key Principles of the Mediterranean Diet

1. **Fresh, Seasonal Ingredients:**
   - Meals are prepared with fresh produce that reflects the seasons, ensuring optimal taste and nutrition.
   - Examples include tomatoes, zucchini, eggplant, and citrus fruits in season.

2. **Whole and Minimally Processed Foods:**
   - The diet avoids heavily processed or refined foods, focusing instead on natural ingredients like whole grains, legumes, and unprocessed meats or fish.

3. **Healthy Fats:**
   - Olive oil is the cornerstone of the diet, used both for cooking and as a dressing.
   - Nuts, seeds, and fatty fish like salmon and sardines are also key sources of beneficial omega-3 fats.

4. **Plant-Based Foundation:**
   - The diet prioritizes plant-based foods, such as fruits, vegetables, whole grains, legumes, and nuts, making it naturally high in fiber and antioxidants.

5. **Moderate Consumption of Animal Products:**
   - Lean proteins, such as fish and poultry, are consumed regularly, while red meat is limited. Dairy products like yogurt and cheese are eaten in moderation.

6. **Herbs and Spices for Flavor:**
   - The use of herbs and spices like oregano, basil, rosemary, and garlic replaces the need for excessive salt, adding layers of flavor and health benefits.

7. **Mindful Eating and Lifestyle:**
   - The Mediterranean Diet encourages slow, mindful meals often shared with family and friends.
   - Physical activity and enjoying life's simple pleasures are integral to the overall approach.

The Mediterranean Diet is not a restrictive eating plan but a celebration of wholesome, flavorful foods and a lifestyle that promotes health, balance, and joy.

2. How to Get Started with the Mediterranean Diet

Embarking on a Mediterranean diet journey can be both exciting and rewarding. This chapter will guide you step by step, making it easy to adopt the principles of this healthy and flavorful lifestyle. Whether you're looking to improve your health, lose weight, or simply enjoy vibrant, wholesome meals, the Mediterranean diet is a sustainable and enjoyable way to achieve your goals.

Step 1: Understand the Core Principles

Before diving in, familiarize yourself with the fundamental aspects of the Mediterranean diet:

- **Focus on Plant-Based Foods:** Make fruits, vegetables, whole grains, legumes, nuts, and seeds the foundation of your meals.
- **Choose Healthy Fats:** Use olive oil as your primary fat source and include fatty fish, avocados, and nuts regularly.
- **Eat Lean Proteins:** Prioritize fish, poultry, and plant-based proteins like lentils and chickpeas. Limit red meat to occasional servings.
- **Embrace Moderation:** Enjoy dairy products, eggs, and wine (if desired) in small amounts.
- **Flavor with Herbs and Spices:** Replace salt with herbs, garlic, lemon, and spices to enhance taste while boosting health benefits.

Step 2: Stock Your Mediterranean Pantry

A well-stocked pantry makes it easier to prepare Mediterranean meals. Here's what to keep on hand:

Staples:
- Extra-virgin olive oil
- Whole grains: quinoa, farro, bulgur, brown rice
- Legumes: chickpeas, lentils, black beans
- Nuts and seeds: almonds, walnuts, sunflower seeds

Spices and Herbs:
- Dried: oregano, thyme, basil, rosemary, paprika
- Fresh: parsley, cilantro, mint, dill

Proteins:
- Canned tuna or salmon
- Frozen fish fillets (salmon, cod, sardines)
- Eggs

Dairy:
- Plain Greek yogurt
- Feta cheese or other aged cheeses

Fresh Produce:
- Seasonal fruits and vegetables (e.g., tomatoes, zucchini, spinach, bell peppers)
- Garlic, onions, and lemons

Other Essentials:
- Whole-grain bread or pita
- Canned tomatoes
- Balsamic or red wine vinegar

Step 3: Plan Your Meals

Transitioning to the Mediterranean diet is easier with a meal plan. Start with simple swaps and gradually build a routine.

1. **Breakfast:** Swap sugary cereals for Greek yogurt topped with nuts, seeds, and fresh fruit.
2. **Lunch:** Prepare a large salad with mixed greens, tomatoes, cucumbers, olives, and grilled chicken or chickpeas.
3. **Dinner:** Opt for dishes like baked fish with roasted vegetables or a hearty lentil stew.
4. **Snacks:** Choose healthy options such as hummus with raw vegetables, a handful of almonds, or fresh fruit.

Step 4: Start with Simple Recipes

Here are a few beginner-friendly recipes to get you started:
- **Greek Salad:** Combine cucumbers, tomatoes, red onion, olives, and feta cheese. Drizzle with olive oil and lemon juice.
- **Mediterranean Bowl:** Layer cooked quinoa, roasted vegetables, grilled chicken, and a dollop of hummus.
- **Lentil Soup:** Sauté onions, carrots, and celery; add lentils, canned tomatoes, and broth; simmer until tender.

Step 5: Make Dining a Joyful Experience

One of the hallmarks of the Mediterranean lifestyle is the emphasis on mindful eating. Enjoy your meals in a relaxed setting, savor each bite, and share meals with loved ones whenever possible. This approach not only enhances satisfaction but also fosters better digestion and overall well-being.

Step 6: Build Healthy Habits Gradually

Adopting a new diet can feel overwhelming, so take it one step at a time:
- Start by incorporating Mediterranean-style meals a few times a week.
- Experiment with new recipes and flavors to keep things exciting.
- Gradually reduce processed foods, refined sugars, and unhealthy fats.

Step 7: Stay Active

The Mediterranean lifestyle isn't just about what you eat—it's also about staying physically active. Incorporate activities you enjoy, such as walking, swimming, or yoga, to complement your new diet and boost your overall health.

Step 8: Track Your Progress

Pay attention to how your body feels as you transition to the Mediterranean diet. Are you feeling more energetic? Are your meals more satisfying? Keep a journal to track your progress, favorite recipes, and any health improvements.

3. What to Eat and What to Avoid on the Mediterranean Diet

The Mediterranean diet is not about strict rules or restrictions but rather a focus on eating wholesome, minimally processed foods that are both delicious and nutritious. This chapter outlines the foods you should include in your diet and those to limit or avoid to reap the full benefits of the Mediterranean lifestyle.

What to Eat on the Mediterranean Diet
The Mediterranean diet emphasizes fresh, nutrient-dense foods that promote health and well-being. These foods are staples in Mediterranean cuisine and should make up the majority of your meals.

Vegetables
- **Why:** Rich in vitamins, minerals, antioxidants, and fiber, vegetables are essential for overall health.
- **Examples:** Tomatoes, zucchini, eggplant, spinach, kale, cucumbers, bell peppers, broccoli, artichokes, and onions.
- **How to Include:** Make vegetables the centerpiece of your meals by incorporating them into salads, soups, and stews or roasting them as a side dish.

Fruits
- **Why:** Packed with natural sugars, fiber, and antioxidants, fruits are a great way to satisfy your sweet tooth while staying healthy.
- **Examples:** Citrus fruits (oranges, lemons), berries, apples, grapes, figs, and pomegranates.
- **How to Include:** Enjoy fresh fruit as a snack, dessert, or addition to salads and yogurt.

Whole Grains

- **Why:** Whole grains provide sustained energy, fiber, and essential nutrients like B vitamins and magnesium.
- **Examples:** Quinoa, farro, bulgur, barley, whole-wheat bread, pasta, and brown rice.
- **How to Include:** Use whole grains as a base for salads, side dishes, or as a hearty main course ingredient.

Healthy Fats

- **Why:** Healthy fats are a cornerstone of the Mediterranean diet, supporting heart health and providing long-lasting energy.
- **Examples:** Extra-virgin olive oil, avocados, nuts (almonds, walnuts), and seeds (sesame, sunflower).
- **How to Include:** Use olive oil for cooking and dressings, snack on nuts and seeds, and add avocado to salads or spreads.

Lean Proteins

- **Why:** High-quality proteins are essential for muscle repair and overall health.
- **Examples:** Fish (salmon, sardines, mackerel), seafood (shrimp, squid, mussels), chicken, turkey, and eggs.
- **How to Include:** Opt for grilled or baked fish and poultry, and include eggs in breakfast or salads.

Legumes

- **Why:** High in fiber, plant-based protein, and essential nutrients, legumes are a Mediterranean staple.
- **Examples:** Chickpeas, lentils, black beans, and kidney beans.
- **How to Include:** Add them to soups, salads, or stews for a hearty and nutritious boost.

Dairy

- **Why:** Provides calcium and protein in moderation.
- **Examples:** Greek yogurt, feta cheese, and Parmesan cheese.
- **How to Include:** Use cheese sparingly as a flavor enhancer and enjoy yogurt as a snack or base for sauces.

Herbs and Spices

- **Why:** Enhance flavor naturally without the need for excessive salt.
- **Examples:** Oregano, basil, rosemary, thyme, parsley, garlic, and mint.
- **How to Include:** Use fresh or dried herbs in marinades, dressings, and main dishes.

Beverages

- **Why:** Hydration and moderation are key.
- **Examples:** Water, herbal teas, and, occasionally, a small glass of red wine.
- **How to Include:** Stay hydrated with water throughout the day, and limit alcohol to one glass of wine with meals if desired.

What to Avoid on the Mediterranean Diet

While the Mediterranean diet is inclusive and flexible, there are certain foods you should limit or avoid to stay aligned with its principles. These foods are often processed, high in unhealthy fats, and lacking in nutritional value.

1. **Highly Processed Foods**
   - **Why:** These foods are loaded with added sugars, unhealthy fats, and artificial ingredients.
   - **Examples:** Chips, packaged snacks, frozen meals, and fast food.
   - **How to Avoid:** Opt for fresh, whole ingredients instead of prepackaged or convenience foods.
2. **Refined Grains**
   - **Why:** Stripped of nutrients and fiber, refined grains can lead to blood sugar spikes.
   - **Examples:** White bread, white rice, and pastries.
   - **How to Avoid:** Replace with whole grains like quinoa, bulgur, and whole-wheat bread.
3. **Sugary Foods and Beverages**
   - **Why:** High sugar intake contributes to weight gain, inflammation, and chronic diseases.
   - **Examples:** Sodas, candy, cakes, cookies, and sweetened cereals.
   - **How to Avoid:** Satisfy your sweet cravings with fresh fruits or small amounts of natural sweeteners like honey.
4. **Red and Processed Meats**
   - **Why:** Linked to heart disease and inflammation when consumed in excess.
   - **Examples:** Bacon, sausage, hot dogs, and processed deli meats.
   - **How to Avoid:** Limit red meat to occasional servings, and replace processed meats with fish or legumes.
5. **Unhealthy Fats**
   - **Why:** Trans fats and saturated fats can increase cholesterol levels and risk of heart disease.
   - **Examples:** Margarine, hydrogenated oils, and fried foods.
   - **How to Avoid:** Stick to healthy fats like olive oil and avoid deep-fried dishes.
6. **Excessive Salt**
   - **Why:** High sodium intake can lead to hypertension and other health issues.
   - **Examples:** Prepackaged soups, canned foods (not low-sodium), and salty snacks.
   - **How to Avoid:** Use herbs, spices, and citrus to flavor meals instead of relying on salt.
7. **Alcohol in Excess**
   - **Why:** While moderate wine consumption is allowed, excessive drinking can negate the health benefits of the Mediterranean diet.
   - **Examples:** Hard liquors, cocktails, and binge drinking.
   - **How to Avoid:** If you drink, limit yourself to one glass of red wine with meals.

Summary: Building Your Mediterranean Plate

What to Load Your Plate With:

- **Half your plate:** Vegetables and fruits.
- **One-quarter:** Whole grains or legumes.
- **One-quarter:** Lean proteins like fish, poultry, or plant-based options.
- **Add healthy fats:** Olive oil, nuts, or avocados.

By focusing on wholesome, nutrient-dense foods and limiting processed, unhealthy options, you'll not only enjoy delicious meals but also promote better health and well-being. The Mediterranean diet is flexible, so adapt it to your preferences and lifestyle while keeping these guidelines in mind.

Final Thoughts

Starting the Mediterranean diet is a journey toward a healthier, more fulfilling lifestyle. By focusing on wholesome foods, enjoying meals with loved ones, and embracing the diet's principles, you'll soon discover how simple and enjoyable it can be to eat well and feel great. Remember, it's not about perfection—it's about progress and creating a way of eating that works for you.

CHAPTER 1: BREAKFASTS TO BRIGHTEN YOUR DAY

1. Greek Yogurt with Honey and Fresh Fruit

Yield: 2 servings **Prep Time:** 5 minutes **Cook Time:** 0 minutes **Cooking Method:** No-cook

Ingredients:
- 2 cups plain Greek yogurt
- 1 tbsp honey
- 1/2 cup mixed fresh fruit (berries, sliced banana, or apple)
- 2 tbsp chopped walnuts

Nutritional Information: 220 calories, 14g protein, 18g carbohydrates, 9g fat, 2g fiber, 10mg cholesterol, 55mg sodium

Directions:
1. Divide the yogurt into two bowls.
2. Drizzle honey evenly over the yogurt.
3. Top with fresh fruit and sprinkle with walnuts.
4. Serve immediately.

2. Avocado Toast with Cherry Tomatoes and Feta

Yield: 2 servings **Prep Time:** 5 minutes **Cook Time:** 5 minutes **Cooking Method:** Toasting

Ingredients:
- 2 slices whole-grain bread
- 1 ripe avocado, sliced
- 1/2 cup cherry tomatoes, halved
- 1 oz crumbled feta cheese
- 1 tsp extra-virgin olive oil
- Pinch of sea salt and black pepper

Nutritional Information: 280 calories, 7g protein, 27g carbohydrates, 17g fat, 5g fiber, 10mg cholesterol, 300mg sodium

Directions:
1. Toast the bread slices.
2. Spread sliced avocado evenly on each slice.
3. Top with cherry tomatoes and feta cheese.
4. Drizzle with olive oil, and season with salt and pepper.

3. Mediterranean Veggie Omelet

Yield: 2 servings   **Prep Time:** 5 minutes   **Cook Time:** 10 minutes   **Cooking Method:** Pan-frying

Ingredients:

- 4 large eggs
- 1/4 cup diced red bell pepper
- 1/4 cup chopped spinach
- 1/4 cup diced tomato
- 1 oz crumbled goat cheese
- 1 tbsp olive oil

Nutritional Information: 240 calories, 15g protein, 6g carbohydrates, 18g fat, 2g fiber, 220mg cholesterol, 300mg sodium

Directions:

1. Whisk eggs in a bowl and set aside.
2. Heat olive oil in a non-stick pan over medium heat. Add bell pepper, spinach, and tomato. Cook for 2-3 minutes.
3. Pour eggs into the pan and cook until the edges set. Sprinkle goat cheese on top.
4. Fold the omelet and cook for another minute. Serve hot.

4. Whole-Grain Porridge with Almond Butter

Yield: 2 servings   **Prep Time:** 5 minutes   **Cook Time:** 10 minutes   **Cooking Method:** Boiling

Ingredients:

- 1 cup rolled oats
- 2 cups almond milk
- 1 tbsp almond butter
- 1 tbsp honey
- 1/4 tsp cinnamon

Nutritional Information: 260 calories, 8g protein, 38g carbohydrates, 9g fat, 4g fiber, 0mg cholesterol, 50mg sodium

Directions:

1. Combine oats and almond milk in a saucepan. Bring to a boil, then reduce to simmer for 5-7 minutes.
2. Stir in almond butter and honey.
3. Sprinkle with cinnamon before serving.
4. Add berries up to your taste.

5. Smoked Salmon and Arugula Wrap

Yield: 2 servings   **Prep Time:** 5 minutes   **Cook Time:** 0 minutes   **Cooking Method:** Assembly

Ingredients:

- 2 whole-grain wraps
- 2 oz smoked salmon
- 1/2 cup arugula
- 2 tbsp light cream cheese
- 1 tsp lemon juice

Nutritional Information: 210 calories, 12g protein, 20g carbohydrates, 9g fat, 2g fiber, 25mg cholesterol, 320mg sodium

Directions:

1. Spread cream cheese on the wraps.
2. Layer smoked salmon and arugula on top.
3. Drizzle with lemon juice, roll tightly, and serve.
4. Add tomatoes up to your taste

6. Zucchini and Feta Breakfast Muffins

Yield: 6 servings   **Prep Time:** 10 minutes   **Cook Time:** 20 minutes   **Cooking Temperature:** 375°F (190°C)   **Cooking Method:** Baking

Ingredients:

- 2 cups grated zucchini
- 1/2 cup whole-wheat flour
- 1/2 cup feta cheese
- 2 large eggs
- 1 tsp baking powder

Nutritional Information: 120 calories, 6g protein, 12g carbohydrates, 6g fat, 2g fiber, 30mg cholesterol, 180mg sodium

Directions:

1. Preheat the oven to 375°F (190°C).
2. Mix zucchini, flour, feta, eggs, and baking powder in a bowl.
3. Divide into a greased muffin tin. Bake for 20 minutes.

7. Spinach and Ricotta Frittata

Yield: 4 servings   **Prep Time:** 5 minutes   **Cook Time:** 15 minutes   **Cooking Temperature:** 350°F (175°C)   **Cooking Method:** Baking

Ingredients:
- 6 large eggs
- 1 cup spinach
- 1/4 cup ricotta cheese
- 1/4 cup diced onion
- 1 tbsp olive oil

Nutritional Information: 190 calories, 14g protein, 3g carbohydrates, 14g fat, 1g fiber, 220mg cholesterol, 260mg sodium

Directions:
1. Preheat the oven to 350°F (175°C).
2. Sauté onion and spinach in olive oil for 3 minutes.
3. Whisk eggs and mix with ricotta. Pour over spinach in an oven-safe skillet. Add cherry tomatoes to your taste
4. Bake for 15 minutes.

8. Mediterranean Breakfast Bowl

Yield: *2 servings*   **Prep Time:** 10 minutes   **Cook Time:** 0 minutes   **Cooking Method:** Assembly

Ingredients:
- 1 cup cooked quinoa (prepared in advance)
- 1/2 cup cherry tomatoes, halved
- 1/4 cup cucumber, diced
- 2 tbsp hummus
- 1 hard-boiled egg, sliced
- 1 tbsp olive oil
- Pinch of paprika

Nutritional Information: 290 calories, 10g protein, 28g carbohydrates, 13g fat, 5g fiber, 185mg cholesterol, 170mg sodium

Directions:
1. Divide quinoa into two bowls.
2. Top with cherry tomatoes, cucumber, hummus, and sliced egg.
3. Drizzle with olive oil and sprinkle paprika on top.

9. Tomato and Spinach Egg White Scramble

Yield: 2 servings   **Prep Time:** 5 minutes   **Cook Time:** 5 minutes   **Cooking Method:** Pan-frying

Ingredients:

- 6 large egg whites
- 1/2 cup spinach
- 1/2 cup diced tomatoes
- 1 tbsp olive oil
- Pinch of salt and pepper

Nutritional Information: 150 calories, 12g protein, 4g carbohydrates, 8g fat, 2g fiber, 0mg cholesterol, 110mg sodium

Directions:

1. Heat olive oil in a pan over medium heat. Add spinach and tomatoes; sauté for 2 minutes.
2. Pour in egg whites and stir gently until cooked through.
3. Season with salt and pepper. Serve warm.

10. Sweet Potato and Avocado Toast

Yield: 2 servings   **Prep Time:** 10 minutes   **Cook Time:** 10 minutes   **Cooking Method:** Baking and Assembly

Ingredients:

- 2 slices baked sweet potato (1/4-inch thick)
- 1 ripe avocado, sliced
- 1/4 tsp chili flakes
- 1 tsp lemon juice

Nutritional Information: 220 calories, 4g protein, 24g carbohydrates, 13g fat, 5g fiber, 0mg cholesterol, 60mg sodium

Directions:

1. Bake sweet potato slices at 400°F (200°C) for 10 minutes or until tender.
2. Spread sliced avocado on the sweet potato slices.
3. Sprinkle with chili flakes and drizzle with lemon juice.

11. Whole-Wheat Pancakes with Honey and Berries

Yield: 4 servings   **Prep Time:** 10 minutes   **Cook Time:** 10 minutes   **Cooking Method:** Pan-frying

Ingredients:
- 1 cup whole-wheat flour
- 1 tsp baking powder
- 1 large egg
- 1 cup almond milk
- 1 tbsp olive oil
- 1 tbsp honey
- 1/2 cup fresh berries

Nutritional Information: 180 calories, 6g protein, 28g carbohydrates, 5g fat, 3g fiber, 25mg cholesterol, 120mg sodium

Directions:
1. Whisk eggs in a bowl and set aside.
2. Heat olive oil in a non-stick pan over medium heat. Add bell pepper, spinach, and tomato. Cook for 2-3 minutes.
3. Pour eggs into the pan and cook until the edges set. Sprinkle goat cheese on top.
4. Fold the omelet and cook for another minute. Serve hot.

12. Caprese Avocado Toast

Yield: 2 servings   **Prep Time:** 5 minutes   **Cook Time:** 5 minutes   **Cooking Method:** Toasting

Ingredients:
- 2 slices whole-grain bread
- 1/2 avocado, sliced
- 4 slices fresh mozzarella
- 4 slices tomato
- 1 tsp balsamic glaze

Nutritional Information: 250 calories, 9g protein, 22g carbohydrates, 14g fat, 3g fiber, 20mg cholesterol, 180mg sodium

Directions:
1. Toast the bread slices.
2. Layer avocado, mozzarella, and tomato on the toast.
3. Drizzle with balsamic glaze. Serve immediately.

13. Mediterranean Chickpea Toast

Yield: 2 servings   **Prep Time:** 5 minutes   **Cook Time:** 0 minutes   **Cooking Method:** No-cook

Ingredients:
- 2 slices whole-grain bread
- 1/2 cup canned chickpeas
- 1 tbsp tahini
- 1 tbsp lemon juice
- 1 tbsp chopped parsley

Nutritional Information: 210 calories, 8g protein, 28g carbohydrates, 8g fat, 5g fiber, 0mg cholesterol, 150mg sodium

Directions:
1. Mix chickpeas with onion, tahini, lemon juice, and parsley.
2. Spread onto toasted bread slices. Serve immediately.

14. Roasted Red Pepper and Goat Cheese Frittata

Yield: 4 servings   **Prep Time:** 10 minutes   **Cook Time:** 20 minutes   **Cooking Temperature:** 375°F (190°C)   **Cooking Method:** Baking

Ingredients:
- 6 large eggs
- 1/2 cup roasted red peppers, chopped
- 1/4 cup goat cheese
- 1/4 cup diced onion
- 1 tbsp olive oil

Nutritional Information: 200 calories, 12g protein, 4g carbohydrates, 15g fat, 1g fiber, 230mg cholesterol, 250mg sodium

Directions:
1. Preheat the oven to 375°F (190°C).
2. Sauté onion in olive oil for 3 minutes. Add red peppers.
3. Whisk eggs and pour into a greased baking dish. Add sautéed vegetables and goat cheese.
4. Bake for 20 minutes or until set.

15. Warm Lentil and Spinach Breakfast Bowl

Yield: 2 servings   **Prep Time:** 5 minutes   **Cook Time:** 10 minutes   **Cooking Method:** Boiling

Ingredients:

- 1 cup cooked lentils
- 1 cup spinach
- 1 tsp olive oil
- 1 tsp lemon juice
- 1 fried egg

Nutritional Information: 220 calories, 12g protein, 22g carbohydrates, 9g fat, 5g fiber, 185mg cholesterol, 150mg sodium

Directions:

1. Heat lentils and spinach in olive oil over medium heat.
2. Divide into bowls and top with a fried egg and few fresh tomatoes.
3. Drizzle with lemon juice before serving.

16. Banana Oat Smoothie

Yield: 2 servings   **Prep Time:** 5 minutes   **Cook Time:** 0 minutes   **Cooking Method:** Blending

Ingredients:

- 1 ripe banana
- 1/2 cup rolled oats
- 1 cup almond milk
- 1 tsp honey
- 1/4 tsp cinnamon

Nutritional Information: 180 calories, 4g protein, 35g carbohydrates, 3g fat, 4g fiber, 0mg cholesterol, 50mg sodium

Directions:

1. Combine all ingredients in a blender.
2. Blend until smooth. Serve immediately.

CHAPTER 2: COLORFUL SALADS AND SATISFYING SOUPS

1. Classic Greek Salad

Yield: 4 servings   **Prep Time:** 10 minutes   **Cook Time:** 0 minutes   **Cooking Method:** No-cook

Ingredients:
- 4 medium tomatoes, diced
- 1 cucumber, sliced
- 1 red onion, thinly sliced
- 1/2 cup Kalamata olives
- 3.5 oz feta cheese, crumbled
- 2 tbsp extra-virgin olive oil
- 1 tbsp red wine vinegar
- 1 tsp dried oregano

Nutritional Information: 200 calories, 5g protein, 12g carbohydrates, 16g fat, 3g fiber, 15mg cholesterol, 260mg sodium

Directions:
1. Combine tomatoes, cucumber, onion, and olives in a large bowl.
2. Drizzle with olive oil and vinegar. Sprinkle with oregano.
3. Gently toss and top with crumbled feta. Serve immediately.

2. Lentil and Spinach Soup

Yield: 6 servings   **Prep Time:** 10 minutes   **Cook Time:** 30 minutes   **Cooking Temperature:** Medium heat   **Cooking Method:** Simmering

Ingredients:
- 1 cup dried green lentils
- 8 cups vegetable broth
- 1 cup diced carrots
- 1 cup diced celery
- 1 onion, diced
- 2 cups fresh spinach
- 2 tbsp olive oil
- 1 tsp ground cumin

Nutritional Information: 190 calories, 8g protein, 26g carbohydrates, 6g fat, 7g fiber, 0mg cholesterol, 320mg sodium

Directions:
1. Heat olive oil in a large pot over medium heat. Sauté carrots, celery, and onion for 5 minutes.
2. Add lentils, broth, and cumin. Simmer for 25 minutes or until lentils are tender.
3. Stir in spinach and cook for 2 minutes. Serve warm.

3. Mediterranean Quinoa Salad

Yield: 4 servings   **Prep Time:** 10 minutes   **Cook Time:** 15 minutes   **Cooking Method:** Boiling

Ingredients:
- 1 cup cooked quinoa
- 1/2 cup diced cucumber
- 1/2 cup cherry tomatoes, halved
- 1/4 cup chopped parsley
- 1/4 cup crumbled feta cheese
- 2 tbsp lemon juice
- 1 tbsp olive oil

Nutritional Information: : 210 calories, 7g protein, 22g carbohydrates, 10g fat, 4g fiber, 10mg cholesterol, 150mg sodium

Directions:
1. Cook quinoa as per package Directions. Cool slightly.
2. Combine all ingredients in a large bowl. Toss with lemon juice and olive oil. Serve chilled or at room temperature.

4. Roasted Tomato Basil Soup

Yield: 4 servings   **Prep Time:** 10 minutes   **Cook Time:** 35 minutes   **Cooking Temperature:** 400°F (200°C)   **Cooking Method:** Roasting and blending

Ingredients:
- 6 medium tomatoes, halved
- 1 onion, quartered
- 4 garlic cloves, peeled
- 3 cups vegetable broth
- 1/4 cup fresh basil leaves
- 2 tbsp olive oil

Nutritional Information: 180 calories, 4g protein, 18g carbohydrates, 10g fat, 4g fiber, 0mg cholesterol, 120mg sodium

Directions:
1. Preheat oven to 400°F (200°C). Toss tomatoes, onion, and garlic with olive oil. Roast for 25 minutes.
2. Blend roasted vegetables with broth and basil until smooth. Heat through and serve.

5. Chickpea and Avocado Salad

Yield: 4 servings   **Prep Time:** 10 minutes   **Cook Time:** 0 minutes   **Cooking Method:** No cook

Ingredients:

- 1 can (15 oz) chickpeas, rinsed and drained
- 1 avocado, diced
- 1/2 cup cherry tomatoes, halved
- 1 tbsp lemon juice
- 1 tbsp olive oil

Nutritional Information: 220 calories, 6g protein, 18g carbohydrates, 14g fat, 7g fiber, 0mg cholesterol, 120mg sodium

Directions:

1. Combine chickpeas, avocado, and tomatoes in a bowl.
2. Drizzle with lemon juice and olive oil. Toss gently. Serve immediately.

6. Moroccan Lentil Soup

Yield: 6 servings   **Prep Time:** 10 minutes   **Cook Time:** 40 minutes   **Cooking Method:** Simmering

Ingredients:

- 1 cup dried lentils
- 8 cups vegetable broth
- 1 cup diced carrots
- 1/2 cup chopped onion
- 1 tbsp ground cumin
- 1 tsp paprika
- 1 tbsp olive oil

Nutritional Information: 180 calories, 9g protein, 28g carbohydrates, 4g fat, 8g fiber, 0mg cholesterol, 200mg sodium

Directions:

1. Heat olive oil in a pot over medium heat. Sauté carrots and onion for 5 minutes.
2. Add lentils, broth, cumin, and paprika. Simmer for 35 minutes. Serve warm.

7. Caprese Salad with Balsamic Glaze

Yield: 4 servings   **Prep Time:** 10 minutes   **Cook Time:** 0 minutes   **Cooking Method:** Assembly

Ingredients:

- 2 medium tomatoes, sliced
- 8 oz fresh mozzarella, sliced
- 1/4 cup fresh basil leaves
- 1 tbsp balsamic glaze
- 1 tbsp olive oil
- Pinch of sea salt and black pepper

Nutritional Information: 210 calories, 10g protein, 7g carbohydrates, 15g fat, 1g fiber, 35mg cholesterol, 150mg sodium

Directions:

1. Arrange tomato slices, mozzarella, and basil leaves alternately on a plate.
2. Drizzle with balsamic glaze and olive oil.
3. Sprinkle with salt and pepper. Serve immediately.

8. Tuscan White Bean and Kale Soup

Yield: 6 servings   **Prep Time:** 10 minutes   **Cook Time:** 25 minutes   **Cooking Temperature:** Medium heat   **Cooking Method:** Simmering

Ingredients:

- 2 cans (15 oz each) cannellini beans, rinsed and drained
- 6 cups vegetable broth
- 2 cups chopped kale
- 1 cup diced carrots
- 1 onion, diced
- 2 garlic cloves, minced
- 1 tbsp olive oil
- 1 tsp dried thyme

Nutritional Information: 190 calories, 9g protein, 27g carbohydrates, 4g fat, 7g fiber, 0mg cholesterol, 200mg sodium

Directions:

1. Heat olive oil in a pot. Sauté onion, garlic, and carrots for 5 minutes.
2. Add beans, broth, thyme, and kale. Simmer for 20 minutes. Serve warm.

9. Roasted Beet and Orange Salad

Yield: 4 servings   **Prep Time:** 10 minutes   **Cook Time:** 30 minutes   **Cooking Temperature:** 400°F (200°C)   **Cooking Method:** Roasting

Ingredients:
- 3 medium beets, peeled and cubed
- 2 oranges, segmented
- 1/4 cup crumbled goat cheese
- 2 tbsp olive oil
- 1 tbsp balsamic vinegar
- 1 tsp honey

Nutritional Information: 220 calories, 6g protein, 22g carbohydrates, 10g fat, 4g fiber, 10mg cholesterol, 80mg sodium

Directions:
1. Preheat oven to 400°F (200°C). Toss beets with 1 tbsp olive oil and roast for 30 minutes.
2. Arrange roasted beets, orange segments, and goat cheese on a plate.
3. Whisk remaining olive oil, balsamic vinegar, and honey. Drizzle over the salad. Serve chilled or at room temperature.

10. Cucumber and Dill Yogurt Soup

Yield: 4 servings   **Prep Time:** 10 minutes   **Cook Time:** 0 minutes   **Cooking Method:** No-cook

Ingredients:
- 2 cups plain Greek yogurt
- 1 cucumber, grated
- 1 clove garlic, minced
- 2 tbsp chopped fresh dill
- 1 tbsp lemon juice

Nutritional Information: 120 calories, 9g protein, 8g carbohydrates, 6g fat, 1g fiber, 5mg cholesterol, 50mg sodium

Directions:
1. In a bowl, combine yogurt, cucumber, garlic, dill, and lemon juice. Mix well.
2. Chill for 10 minutes before serving.

11. Grilled Eggplant Salad

Yield: 4 servings **Prep Time:** 10 minutes **Cook Time:** 10 minutes **Cooking Temperature:** Medium heat **Cooking Method:** Grilling

Ingredients:

- 1 large eggplant, sliced
- 1/2 cup cherry tomatoes, halved
- 2 tbsp olive oil
- 1 tbsp balsamic vinegar
- 1 tbsp chopped parsley

Nutritional Information: 140 calories, 2g protein, 10g carbohydrates, 10g fat, 3g fiber, 0mg cholesterol, 40mg sodium

Directions:

1. Brush eggplant slices with olive oil. Grill for 3-4 minutes on each side.
2. Arrange grilled eggplant and cherry tomatoes on a plate. Drizzle with balsamic vinegar and sprinkle parsley.

12. Zucchini Noodle and Pesto Salad

Yield: 4 servings **Prep Time:** 10 minutes **Cook Time:** 0 minutes **Cooking Method:** No-cook

Ingredients:

- 2 medium zucchinis, spiralized
- 2 tbsp pesto
- 1/4 cup cherry tomatoes, halved
- 1 tbsp pine nuts

Nutritional Information: 180 calories, 5g protein, 10g carbohydrates, 14g fat, 2g fiber, 5mg cholesterol, 50mg sodium

Directions:

1. Toss zucchini noodles with pesto in a large bowl.
2. Add cherry tomatoes and sprinkle with pine nuts. Serve chilled.

13. Gazpacho

Yield: 4 servings   **Prep Time:** 15 minutes   **Cook Time:** 0 minutes   **Cooking Method:**Blending

Ingredients:
- 6 ripe tomatoes
- 1 cucumber, peeled
- 1 red bell pepper
- 1 clove garlic
- 2 tbsp olive oil
- 1 tbsp red wine vinegar

Nutritional Information: 150 calories, 2g protein, 12g carbohydrates, 10g fat, 2g fiber, 0mg cholesterol, 80mg sodium

Directions:
1. Combine all ingredients in a blender and blend until smooth.
2. Chill for 1 hour before serving.

14. Chickpea and Roasted Pepper Salad

Yield: 4 servings   **Prep Time:** 10 minutes   **Cook Time:** 15 minutes   **Cooking Method:** Roasting

Ingredients:
- 1 can (15 oz) chickpeas, rinsed and drained
- 2 red bell peppers, roasted and sliced
- 1 tbsp olive oil
- 1 tbsp lemon juice

Nutritional Information: 180 calories, 6g protein, 18g carbohydrates, 8g fat, 6g fiber, 0mg cholesterol, 80mg sodium

Directions:
1. Roast red peppers at 400°F (200°C) for 15 minutes.
2. Combine chickpeas, roasted peppers, olive oil, and lemon juice. Toss gently.

15. Warm Barley and Vegetable Salad

Yield: 4 servings   **Prep Time:** 10 minutes   **Cook Time:** 20 minutes   **Cooking Method:**Simmering

Ingredients:
- 1 cup cooked barley
- 1 cup diced zucchini
- 1/2 cup cherry tomatoes
- 1 tbsp olive oil
- 1 tsp dried oregano

Nutritional Information: 190 calories, 5g protein, 35g carbohydrates, 6g fat, 5g fiber, 0mg cholesterol, 50mg sodium

Directions:
1. Cook barley as per package Directions.
2. Sauté zucchini in olive oil for 5 minutes. Mix with barley, tomatoes, and oregano. Serve warm.

16. Lemon Lentil Soup

Yield: 6 servings   **Prep Time:** 10 minutes   **Cook Time:** 20 minutes   **Cooking Method:** Simmering

Ingredients:
- 1 cup red lentils
- 8 cups vegetable broth
- 1 onion, diced
- 2 tbsp lemon juice
- 1 tbsp olive oil

Nutritional Information: 170 calories, 9g protein, 25g carbohydrates, 4g fat, 6g fiber, 0mg cholesterol, 200mg sodium

Directions:
1. Heat olive oil and sauté onion for 5 minutes.
2. Add lentils, broth, and lemon juice. Simmer for 30 minutes. Serve warm.

CHAPTER 3: LIGHT AND FLAVORFUL LUNCHES

1. Grilled Chicken and Vegetable Wraps

Yield: 4 servings   **Prep Time:** 10 minutes   **Cook Time:** 10 minutes   **Cooking Method:** Grilling

Ingredients:

- 2 medium chicken breasts, sliced thin
- 1 zucchini, sliced lengthwise
- 1 red bell pepper, sliced into strips
- 4 whole-grain wraps
- 2 tbsp olive oil
- 1/4 cup hummus
- 1 tsp dried oregano

Nutritional Information: 290 calories, 22g protein, 25g carbohydrates, 9g fat, 4g fiber, 45mg cholesterol, 300mg sodium

Directions:

1. Brush chicken and vegetables with olive oil and sprinkle with oregano. Grill for 3-4 minutes on each side until cooked.
2. Spread hummus on wraps, layer grilled chicken and vegetables, then roll tightly. Serve warm.

2. Mediterranean Tuna Salad

Yield: 2 servings   **Prep Time:** 10 minutes   **Cook Time:** 0 minutes   **Cooking Method:** No-cook

Ingredients:

- 1 can (5 oz) tuna, packed in olive oil, drained
- 1/2 cup cherry tomatoes, halved
- 1/4 cup diced onion
- 2 tbsp Kalamata olives, sliced
- 1 tbsp lemon juice
- 1 tbsp olive oil

Nutritional Information: 220 calories, 20g protein, 5g carbohydrates, 12g fat, 1g fiber, 30mg cholesterol, 350mg sodium

Directions:

1. Combine tuna, tomatoes, onion, and olives in a bowl.
2. Drizzle with lemon juice and olive oil, then toss gently. Serve immediately.

3. Chickpea and Spinach Stir-Fry

Yield: 4 servings   **Prep Time:** 15 minutes   **Cook Time:** 10minutes   **Cooking Method:** Sautéing

Ingredients:
- 1 can (15 oz) chickpeas, rinsed and drained
- 4 cups fresh spinach
- 1 small onion, diced
- 2 tbsp olive oil
- 1 clove garlic, minced

Nutritional Information: 180 calories, 6g protein, 18g carbohydrates, 8g fat, 5g fiber, 0mg cholesterol, 200mg sodium

Directions:
1. Heat olive oil in a skillet over medium heat. Add onion and garlic, sauté for 2 minutes.
2. Stir in chickpeas and spinach. Cook until spinach wilts, about 5 minutes. Serve warm.

4. Caprese Stuffed Portobello Mushrooms

Yield: 4 servings   **Prep Time:** 10 minutes   **Cook Time:** 15 minutes   **Cooking Temperature:** 375°F (190°C)   **Cooking Method:** Baking

Ingredients:
- 4 large Portobello mushrooms
- 4 slices fresh mozzarella
- 1 tomato, sliced
- 2 tbsp balsamic glaze
- 1 tbsp olive oil

Nutritional Information: 170 calories, 7g protein, 8g carbohydrates, 12g fat, 2g fiber, 15mg cholesterol, 120mg sodium

Directions:
1. Preheat oven to 375°F (190°C). Brush mushrooms with olive oil and bake for 10 minutes.
2. Top each mushroom with mozzarella and tomato slices, then bake for 5 more minutes. Drizzle with balsamic glaze before serving.

5. Shrimp and Avocado Salad

Yield: 2 servings   **Prep Time:** 5 minutes   **Cook Time:** 10 minutes   **Cooking Method:** Sautéing

Ingredients:

- 8 oz shrimp, peeled and deveined
- 1 avocado, diced
- 1/2 cup cherry tomatoes, halved
- 1 tbsp olive oil
- 1 tbsp lemon juice

Nutritional Information: 250 calories, 20g protein, 8g carbohydrates, 16g fat, 3g fiber, 115mg cholesterol, 250mg sodium

Directions:

1. Heat olive oil in a skillet over medium heat. Sauté shrimp for 3-4 minutes or until cooked.
2. Combine shrimp, avocado, and cherry tomatoes in a bowl. Drizzle with lemon juice.

6. Lemon Orzo with Asparagus

Yield: 4 servings   **Prep Time:** 10 minutes   **Cook Time:** 15 minutes   **Cooking Method:** Boiling

Ingredients:

- 1 cup orzo pasta
- 1 cup asparagus, chopped
- 2 tbsp lemon juice
- 1 tbsp olive oil

Nutritional Information: 220 calories, 7g protein, 34g carbohydrates, 6g fat, 3g fiber, 0mg cholesterol, 50mg sodium

Directions:

1. Cook orzo as per package Directions. Add asparagus in the last 2 minutes of cooking. Drain.
2. Toss with lemon juice and olive oil. Serve warm.

7. Grilled Vegetable and Hummus Wrap

Yield: 2 servings **Prep Time:** 10 minutes **Cook Time:** 10 minutes **Cooking Method:** Grilling

Ingredients:

- 1 zucchini, sliced lengthwise
- 1 red bell pepper, sliced
- 1 eggplant, sliced
- 4 whole-grain wraps
- 1/2 cup hummus
- 1 tbsp olive oil

Nutritional Information: 240 calories, 6g protein, 32g carbohydrates, 10g fat, 5g fiber, 0mg cholesterol, 120mg sodium

Directions:

1. Brush vegetables with olive oil and grill for 3-4 minutes on each side.
2. Spread hummus on wraps, layer grilled vegetables, roll tightly, and serve.

8. Mediterranean Chicken Salad Bowl

Yield: 4 servings **Prep Time:** 15 minutes **Cook Time:** 10 minutes **Cooking Method:** Grilling

Ingredients:

- 2 medium chicken breasts
- 1 cup cherry tomatoes, halved
- 1 cucumber, diced
- 4 cups mixed greens
- 2 tbsp olive oil
- 1 tbsp balsamic vinegar

Nutritional Information: 280 calories, 30g protein, 8g carbohydrates, 12g fat, 3g fiber, 60mg cholesterol, 200mg sodium

Directions:

1. Grill chicken for 5 minutes per side or until cooked through. Slice thinly.
2. Arrange mixed greens, tomatoes, cucumber, and chicken in bowls. Drizzle with olive oil and balsamic vinegar.

9. Tomato and Feta Stuffed Peppers

Yield: 4 servings   **Prep Time:** 10 minutes   **Cook Time:** 20 minutes   **Cooking Temperature:** 375°F (190°C)   **Cooking Method:** Baking

Ingredients:
- 4 bell peppers, halved and seeds removed
- 1 cup cherry tomatoes, halved
- 1/4 cup crumbled feta cheese
- 1 tbsp olive oil
- 1 tsp dried oregano

Nutritional Information: 180 calories, 6g protein, 14g carbohydrates, 11g fat, 3g fiber, 15mg cholesterol, 100mg sodium

Directions:
1. Preheat oven to 375°F (190°C). Place peppers on a baking tray.
2. Mix tomatoes, feta, olive oil, and oregano. Stuff mixture into peppers. Bake for 20 minutes.

10. Mediterranean Chickpea Buddha Bowl

Yield: 4 servings   **Prep Time:** 10 minutes   **Cook Time:** 5 minutes   **Cooking Method:** Sautéing

Ingredients:
- 1 can (15 oz) chickpeas, rinsed and drained
- 2 cups cooked quinoa
- 1 cup cherry tomatoes, halved
- 1 avocado, sliced
- 2 tbsp tahini
- 1 tbsp olive oil

Nutritional Information: 320 calories, 10g protein, 35g carbohydrates, 15g fat, 6g fiber, 0mg cholesterol, 200mg sodium

Directions:
1. Sauté chickpeas in olive oil for 5 minutes.
2. Divide quinoa, chickpeas, tomatoes, and avocado into bowls. Drizzle with tahini before serving.

11. Grilled Salmon with Lemon and Dill

Yield: 4 servings **Prep Time:** 10 minutes **Cook Time:** 10 minutes **Cooking Temperature:** Medium-high heat **Cooking Method:** Grilling

Ingredients:
- 4 salmon fillets (4 oz each)
- 2 tbsp olive oil
- 1 tbsp lemon juice
- 1 tsp dried dill

Nutritional Information: 290 calories, 26g protein, 0g carbohydrates, 20g fat, 0g fiber, 55mg cholesterol, 180mg sodium

Directions:
1. Brush salmon with olive oil, lemon juice, and dill.
2. Grill for 4-5 minutes per side or until cooked through. Serve warm.

12. Warm Farro and Roasted Vegetable Salad

Yield: 4 servings **Prep Time:** 10 minutes **Cook Time:** 25 minutes **Cooking Temperature:** 400°F (200°C) **Cooking Method:** Roasting

Ingredients:
- 1 cup cooked farro
- 1 zucchini, diced
- 1 red bell pepper, diced
- 1 cup cherry tomatoes, halved
- 2 tbsp olive oil

Nutritional Information: 230 calories, 6g protein, 34g carbohydrates, 8g fat, 4g fiber, 0mg cholesterol, 60mg sodium

Directions:
1. Preheat oven to 400°F (200°C). Toss vegetables with olive oil and roast for 20-25 minutes.
2. Combine roasted vegetables with farro. Serve warm or at room temperature.

13. Zucchini Noodle and Shrimp Bowl

Yield: 2 servings   **Prep Time:** 10 minutes   **Cook Time:** 5 minutes   **Cooking Method:** Sautéing

Ingredients:
- 2 medium zucchinis, spiralized
- 8 oz shrimp, peeled and deveined
- 2 tbsp olive oil
- 1 clove garlic, minced

Nutritional Information: 190 calories, 20g protein, 6g carbohydrates, 10g fat, 2g fiber, 115mg cholesterol, 150mg sodium

Directions:
1. Heat olive oil in a skillet over medium heat. Sauté garlic and shrimp for 3-4 minutes.
2. Add zucchini noodles and toss for 1 minute. Serve warm.

14. Mediterranean Egg Salad

Yield: 4 servings   **Prep Time:** 10 minutes   **Cook Time:** 10 minutes   **Cooking Method:** Boiling

Ingredients:
- 6 hard-boiled eggs, chopped
- 1/4 cup plain Greek yogurt
- 1 tbsp Dijon mustard
- 1 tbsp olive oil
- 1/4 cup chopped parsley

Nutritional Information: 170 calories, 12g protein, 2g carbohydrates, 12g fat, 1g fiber, 185mg cholesterol, 150mg sodium

Directions:
1. Mix eggs, yogurt, mustard, olive oil, and parsley in a bowl.
2. Serve on whole-grain bread or as a lettuce wrap.

15. Roasted Cauliflower and Chickpea Bowl

Yield: 4 servings   **Prep Time:** 10 minutes   **Cook Time:** 25 minutes   **Cooking Temperature:** 400°F (200°C)   **Cooking Method:** Roasting

Ingredients:

- 1 head cauliflower, cut into florets
- 1 can (15 oz) chickpeas, rinsed and drained
- 2 tbsp olive oil
- 1 tsp smoked paprika
- ½ Sliced onion and tomato

Nutritional Information: 210 calories, 7g protein, 18g carbohydrates, 10g fat, 6g fiber, 0mg cholesterol, 120mg sodium

Directions:

1. Preheat oven to 400°F (200°C). Toss cauliflower and chickpeas with olive oil, onion, tomato and paprika. Roast for 25 minutes.
2. Serve warm with a drizzle of tahini if desired.

16. Grilled Halloumi and Vegetable Salad

Yield: 4 servings   **Prep Time:** 10 minutes   **Cook Time:** 10 minutes   **Cooking Method:** Grilling

Ingredients:

- 8 oz halloumi cheese, sliced
- 2 cups arugula
- 1 cup cherry tomatoes, halved
- 1 tbsp olive oil

Nutritional Information: 250 calories, 12g protein, 6g carbohydrates, 20g fat, 2g fiber, 25mg cholesterol, 400mg sodium

Directions:

1. Grill halloumi for 2 minutes on each side.
2. Arrange arugula, cherry tomatoes, and halloumi on a plate. Drizzle with olive oil.

CHAPTER 4: WHOLESOME MAINS FOR DINNER

1. Herb-Crusted Baked Cod

Yield: 4 servings **Prep Time:** 10 minutes **Cook Time:** 15 minutes **Cooking Temperature:** 375°F (190°C) **Cooking Method:** Baking

Ingredients:
- 4 cod fillets (6 oz each)
- 1/2 cup whole-wheat breadcrumbs
- 1 tbsp fresh parsley, chopped
- 1 clove garlic, minced
- 1 tbsp olive oil
- 1 tbsp lemon juice

Nutritional Information: 220 calories, 30g protein, 6g carbohydrates, 8g fat, 1g fiber, 55mg cholesterol, 220mg sodium

Directions:
1. Preheat oven to 375°F (190°C).
2. Mix breadcrumbs, parsley, garlic, and olive oil in a bowl.
3. Brush cod fillets with lemon juice, then coat with the breadcrumb mixture.
4. Place fillets on a baking sheet and bake for 15 minutes or until the fish flakes easily with a fork.

2. Greek-Style Grilled Chicken with Tzatziki

Yield: 4 servings **Prep Time:** 15 minutes **Cook Time:** 10 minutes **Cooking Method:** Grilling

Ingredients:
- 4 boneless, skinless chicken breasts
- 2 tbsp olive oil
- 1 tbsp dried oregano
- 2 tbsp lemon juice
- 1 cup plain Greek yogurt
- 1 clove garlic, minced
- 1 cucumber, grated

Nutritional Information: 250 calories, 35g protein, 3g carbohydrates, 10g fat, 1g fiber, 85mg cholesterol, 180mg sodium

Directions:
1. Marinate chicken in olive oil, oregano, and lemon juice for 15 minutes.
2. Grill chicken for 5-6 minutes per side or until fully cooked.
3. Mix yogurt, garlic, and grated cucumber to make tzatziki sauce. Serve chicken with sauce.

3. Mediterranean Stuffed Bell Peppers

Yield: 4 servings **Prep Time:** 10 minutes **Cook Time:** 30 minutes **Cooking Temperature:** 375°F (190°C) **Cooking Method:** Baking

Ingredients:

- 4 large bell peppers, halved and seeds removed
- 1 cup cooked quinoa
- 1 cup diced tomatoes
- 1/2 cup crumbled feta cheese
- 1 tbsp olive oil
- 1 tsp dried oregano

Nutritional Information: 200 calories, 8g protein, 22g carbohydrates, 8g fat, 4g fiber, 10mg cholesterol, 150mg sodium

Directions:

1. Preheat oven to 375°F (190°C). Arrange bell peppers on a baking tray.
2. Mix quinoa, tomatoes, feta, olive oil, and oregano. Stuff into peppers.
3. Bake for 30 minutes. Serve warm.

4. Lemon Herb Grilled Salmon

Yield: 4 servings **Prep Time:** 10 minutes **Cook Time:** 10 minutes **Cooking Method:** Grilling

Ingredients:

- 4 salmon fillets (6 oz each)
- 2 tbsp olive oil
- 1 tbsp lemon juice
- 1 tsp dried dill

Nutritional Information: 300 calories, 25g protein, 0g carbohydrates, 20g fat, 0g fiber, 55mg cholesterol, 200mg sodium

Directions:

1. Brush salmon with olive oil, lemon juice, and dill.
2. Grill for 4-5 minutes per side or until cooked through. Serve warm.

5. One-Pan Mediterranean Chicken and Vegetables

Yield: 4 servings   **Prep Time:** 10 minutes   **Cook Time:** 25 minutes   **Cooking Temperature:** 400°F (200°C)   **Cooking Method:** Roasting

Ingredients:
- 4 chicken thighs, bone-in, skin removed
- 1 zucchini, diced
- 1 red bell pepper, diced
- 1/2 cup cherry tomatoes
- 2 tbsp olive oil
- 1 tsp paprika

Nutritional Information: 310 calories, 25g protein, 6g carbohydrates, 18g fat, 2g fiber, 90mg cholesterol, 150mg sodium

Directions:
1. Preheat oven to 400°F (200°C). Arrange chicken and vegetables on a baking tray.
2. Drizzle with olive oil and sprinkle with paprika. Roast for 25 minutes or until chicken is cooked through.

6. Shrimp and Spinach Orzo

Yield: 4 servings   **Prep Time:** 10 minutes   **Cook Time:** 15 minutes   **Cooking Method:** Boiling and sautéing

Ingredients:
- 1 cup orzo pasta
- 8 oz shrimp, peeled and deveined
- 2 cups spinach
- 2 tbsp olive oil
- 1 clove garlic, minced

Nutritional Information: 290 calories, 18g protein, 32g carbohydrates, 10g fat, 2g fiber, 120mg cholesterol, 150mg sodium

Directions:
1. Cook orzo according to package Directions. Drain and set aside.
2. Heat olive oil in a skillet. Sauté garlic and shrimp for 4 minutes. Add spinach and cook until wilted.
3. Toss with orzo and serve.

7. Ratatouille with Chickpeas

Yield: 4 servings   **Prep Time:** 10 minutes   **Cook Time:** 20 minutes   **Cooking Method:** *Simmering*

Ingredients:

- 1 zucchini, diced
- 1 eggplant, diced
- 1 red bell pepper, diced
- 1 can (15 oz) chickpeas, rinsed and drained
- 2 cups diced tomatoes
- 2 tbsp olive oil
- 1 tsp dried thyme

Nutritional Information: 220 calories, 6g protein, 26g carbohydrates, 10g fat, 7g fiber, 0mg cholesterol, 200mg sodium

Directions:

1. Heat olive oil in a large skillet. Sauté zucchini, eggplant, and bell pepper for 5 minutes.
2. Add chickpeas, tomatoes, and thyme. Simmer for 25 minutes, stirring occasionally. Serve warm.

8. Grilled Swordfish with Olive Tapenade

Yield: 4 servings   **Prep Time:** 10 minutes   **Cook Time:** 10 minutes   **Cooking Method:** Grilling

Ingredients:

- 4 swordfish steaks (6 oz each)
- 2 tbsp olive oil
- 1/4 cup black olive tapenade
- 1 tbsp lemon juice

Nutritional Information: 320 calories, 32g protein, 2g carbohydrates, 20g fat, 0g fiber, 80mg cholesterol, 200mg sodium

Directions:

1. Brush swordfish with olive oil and grill for 4-5 minutes per side.
2. Serve topped with olive tapenade and a squeeze of lemon juice.

9. Stuffed Eggplant with Ground Turkey

Yield: 4 servings   **Prep Time:** 15 minutes   **Cook Time:** 30 minutes   **Cooking Temperature:** 375°F (190°C)   **Cooking Method:** Baking

Ingredients:
- 2 medium eggplants, halved and scooped out
- 8 oz ground turkey
- 1 cup diced tomatoes
- 1/4 cup chopped onion
- 2 tbsp olive oil
- 1 tsp ground cumin

Nutritional Information: 280 calories, 25g protein, 12g carbohydrates, 14g fat, 4g fiber, 70mg cholesterol, 180mg sodium

Directions:
1. Preheat oven to 375°F (190°C). Sauté turkey, onion, and cumin in olive oil until browned.
2. Mix in tomatoes. Fill eggplant halves with the turkey mixture.
3. Bake for 30 minutes.

10. Baked Cod with Cherry Tomatoes and Olives

Yield: 4 servings   **Prep Time:** 10 minutes   **Cook Time:** 20 minutes   **Cooking Temperature:** 375°F (190°C)   **Cooking Method:** Baking

Ingredients:
- 4 cod fillets (6 oz each)
- 1 cup cherry tomatoes, halved
- 1/4 cup Kalamata olives, sliced
- 2 tbsp olive oil
- 1 tbsp lemon juice

Nutritional Information: 220 calories, 30g protein, 4g carbohydrates, 8g fat, 1g fiber, 55mg cholesterol, 200mg sodium

Directions:
1. Preheat oven to 375°F (190°C). Arrange cod, tomatoes, and olives in a baking dish.
2. Drizzle with olive oil and lemon juice. Bake for 20 minutes or until fish flakes easily.

11. Chicken Souvlaki Skewers

Yield: 4 servings   **Prep Time:** 15 minutes   **Cook Time:** 10 minutes   **Cooking Method:** Grilling

Ingredients:

- 2 medium chicken breasts, cubed
- 2 tbsp olive oil
- 1 tbsp lemon juice
- 1 tsp dried oregano

Nutritional Information: 230 calories, 26g protein, 1g carbohydrates, 13g fat, 0g fiber, 70mg cholesterol, 120mg sodium

Directions:

1. Marinate chicken in olive oil, lemon juice, and oregano for 15 minutes.
2. Thread onto skewers with diced onion and tomatoes and grill for 4-5 minutes per side. Serve warm.

12. Spinach and Feta Stuffed Chicken Breasts

Yield: 4 servings   **Prep Time:** 10 minutes   **Cook Time:** 25 minutes   **Cooking Temperature:** 375°F (190°C)   **Cooking Method:** Baking

Ingredients:

- 4 boneless chicken breasts
- 1/2 cup spinach, chopped
- 1/4 cup crumbled feta cheese
- 1 tbsp olive oil

Nutritional Information: 260 calories, 30g protein, 2g carbohydrates, 14g fat, 1g fiber, 85mg cholesterol, 150mg sodium

Directions:

1. Preheat oven to 375°F (190°C). Slice a pocket into each chicken breast.
2. Stuff with spinach, few cherry tomatoes and feta. Secure with toothpicks.
3. Brush with olive oil and bake for 25 minutes.

13. Zucchini and Tomato Pasta

Yield: 4 servings   **Prep Time:** 10 minutes   **Cook Time:** 15 minutes   **Cooking Method:** Boiling and sautéing

Ingredients:

- 8 oz whole-grain spaghetti
- 1 zucchini, sliced
- 1 cup cherry tomatoes, halved
- 2 tbsp olive oil
- 1 clove garlic, minced

Nutritional Information: 290 calories, 8g protein, 42g carbohydrates, 10g fat, 5g fiber, 0mg cholesterol, 120mg sodium

Directions:

1. Cook spaghetti as per package Directions. Drain.
2. Sauté garlic, zucchini, and tomatoes in olive oil for 5 minutes. Toss with pasta and serve.

14. Roasted Cauliflower Steak with Tahini Sauce

Yield: 4 servings   **Prep Time:** 10 minutes   **Cook Time:** 25 minutes   **Cooking Temperature:** 400°F (200°C)   **Cooking Method:** Roasting

Ingredients:

- 1 large cauliflower, sliced into steaks
- 2 tbsp olive oil
- 1 tsp smoked paprika
- 1/4 cup tahini

Nutritional Information: 190 calories, 6g protein, 14g carbohydrates, 12g fat, 5g fiber, 0mg cholesterol, 80mg sodium

Directions:

1. Preheat oven to 400°F (200°C). Brush cauliflower with olive oil and paprika. Roast for 25 minutes.
2. Drizzle with tahini before serving.

15. Baked Tilapia with Lemon and Garlic

Yield: 4 servings   **Prep Time:** 10 minutes   **Cook Time:** 20 minutes   **Cooking Temperature:** 375°F (190°C)   **Cooking Method:** Baking

Ingredients:
- 4 tilapia fillets (6 oz each)
- 2 tbsp olive oil
- 2 cloves garlic, minced
- 1 tbsp lemon juice

Nutritional Information: 200 calories, 35g protein, 0g carbohydrates, 7g fat, 0g fiber, 50mg cholesterol, 100mg sodium

Directions:
1. Preheat oven to 375°F (190°C). Arrange tilapia in a baking dish.
2. Mix olive oil, garlic, and lemon juice. Drizzle over fish. Bake for 20 minutes.

16. Eggplant and Lentil Stew

Yield: 4 servings   **Prep Time:** 10 minutes   **Cook Time:** 30 minutes   **Cooking Method:** Simmering

Ingredients:
- 1 eggplant, diced
- 1 cup dried lentils
- 2 cups diced tomatoes
- 1 cup vegetable broth
- 1 tbsp olive oil

Nutritional Information: 240 calories, 12g protein, 30g carbohydrates, 8g fat, 8g fiber, 0mg cholesterol, 150mg sodium

Directions:
1. Heat olive oil in a pot. Sauté eggplant for 5 minutes.
2. Add lentils, tomatoes, and broth. Simmer for 25 minutes or until lentils are tender.

CHAPTER 5: SNACKS AND SMALL PLATES (MEZZE)

1. Classic Hummus

Yield: 4 servings | **Prep Time:** 10 minutes | **Cook Time:** 0 minutes | **Cooking Method:** Blending

Ingredients:
- 1 can (15 oz) chickpeas, rinsed and drained
- 2 tbsp tahini
- 2 tbsp lemon juice
- 2 cloves garlic
- 2 tbsp extra-virgin olive oil
- 1/4 tsp ground cumin

Nutritional Information: 180 calories, 6g protein, 16g carbohydrates, 10g fat, 4g fiber, 0mg cholesterol, 180mg sodium

Directions:
1. Combine all ingredients in a blender or food processor. Blend until smooth.
2. Adjust consistency with water if needed. Serve with whole-grain pita or vegetable sticks.

2. Tzatziki Dip

Yield: 4 servings | **Prep Time:** 10 minutes | **Cook Time:** 0 minutes | **Cooking Method:** No-cook

Ingredients:
- 1 cup plain Greek yogurt
- 1/2 cucumber, grated
- 1 clove garlic, minced
- 1 tbsp lemon juice
- 1 tbsp fresh dill, chopped

Nutritional Information: 90 calories, 8g protein, 4g carbohydrates, 5g fat, 1g fiber, 5mg cholesterol, 50mg sodium

Directions:
1. Combine all ingredients in a bowl. Mix well.
2. Chill for 10 minutes before serving with raw veggies or pita bread.

3. Stuffed Grape Leaves (Dolmas)

Yield: 4 servings   **Prep Time:** 20 minutes   **Cook Time:** 30 minutes   **Cooking Method:** Simmering

Ingredients:
- 20 grape leaves (jarred or fresh)
- 1/2 cup cooked rice
- 1/4 cup diced onion
- 1 tbsp pine nuts
- 1 tbsp olive oil
- 1 tbsp lemon juice

Nutritional Information: 120 calories, 2g protein, 12g carbohydrates, 7g fat, 1g fiber, 0mg cholesterol, 80mg sodium

Directions:
1. Mix rice, onion, pine nuts, olive oil, and lemon juice.
2. Place 1 tsp filling on each grape leaf. Roll tightly.
3. Simmer in water or broth for 30 minutes. Serve warm or chilled.

4. Marinated Olives

Yield: 4 servings   **Prep Time:** 5 minutes   **Cook Time:** 0 minutes   **Cooking Method:** No-cook

Ingredients:
- 1 cup mixed olives
- 1 tbsp olive oil
- 1/2 tsp dried oregano
- 1 clove garlic, minced

Nutritional Information: 120 calories, 1g protein, 2g carbohydrates, 11g fat, 0g fiber, 0mg cholesterol, 220mg **sodium**

Directions:
1. Toss olives with olive oil, oregano, and garlic.
2. Let marinate for 10 minutes before serving.

5. Baked Falafel

Yield: 4 servings   **Prep Time:** 15 minutes   **Cook Time:** 25 minutes   **Cooking Temperature:** 375°F (190°C)   **Cooking Method:** Baking

Ingredients:
- 1 can (15 oz) chickpeas, rinsed and drained
- 1/4 cup chopped parsley
- 1 clove garlic
- 1 tbsp olive oil
- 1 tsp ground cumin

Nutritional Information: 150 calories, 5g protein, 15g carbohydrates, 7g fat, 4g fiber, 0mg cholesterol, 180mg sodium

Directions:
1. Preheat oven to 375°F (190°C). Blend chickpeas, parsley, garlic, olive oil, and cumin in a food processor.
2. Form into small patties and place on a baking sheet. Bake for 25 minutes, flipping halfway through.

6. Grilled Halloumi Skewers

Yield: 4 servings   **Prep Time:** 10 minutes   **Cook Time:** 5 minutes   **Cooking Method:** Grilling

Ingredients:
- 8 oz halloumi cheese, cubed
- 1 zucchini, sliced
- 1 red bell pepper, diced
- 1 tbsp olive oil

Nutritional Information: 12g protein, 4g carbohydrates, 16g fat, 1g fiber, 25mg cholesterol, 320mg sodium

Directions:
1. Thread halloumi, zucchini, and bell pepper onto skewers. Brush with olive oil.
2. Grill for 2-3 minutes per side. Serve warm.

7. Roasted Red Pepper Dip (Muhammara)

Yield: 4 servings   **Prep Time:** 10 minutes   **Cook Time:** 5 minutes   **Cooking Method:** Blending

Ingredients:

- 2 roasted red peppers
- 1/4 cup walnuts
- 2 tbsp olive oil
- 1 tbsp lemon juice
- 1 clove garlic

Nutritional Information: 160 calories, 3g protein, 8g carbohydrates, 14g fat, 2g fiber, 0mg cholesterol, 60mg sodium

Directions:

1. Blend all ingredients in a food processor until smooth.
2. Serve with pita chips or raw vegetables.

8. Spiced Lentil Patties

Yield: 4 servings   **Prep Time:** 10 minutes   **Cook Time:** 20 minutes   **Cooking Method:** Pan-frying

Ingredients:

- 1 cup cooked lentils
- 1/4 cup breadcrumbs
- 1 egg
- 1 clove garlic, minced
- 1 tsp ground cumin

Nutritional Information: 190 calories, 8g protein, 20g carbohydrates, 8g fat, 4g fiber, 20mg cholesterol, 150mg sodium

Directions:

1. Mix lentils, breadcrumbs, egg, garlic, and cumin. Form into small patties.
2. Pan-fry in olive oil for 2-3 minutes per side. Serve warm.

9. Spinach and Feta Phyllo Triangles

Yield: 6 servings   **Prep Time:** 20 minutes   **Cook Time:** 25 minutes   **Cooking Temperature:** 375°F (190°C)   **Cooking Method:** Baking

Ingredients:
- 1 cup fresh spinach, chopped
- 1/2 cup crumbled feta cheese
- 6 sheets phyllo dough
- 2 tbsp olive oil

Nutritional Information: 150 calories, 5g protein, 10g carbohydrates, 10g fat, 1g fiber, 15mg cholesterol, 200mg sodium

Directions:
1. Preheat oven to 375°F (190°C). Sauté spinach in 1 tbsp olive oil until wilted. Mix with feta cheese.
2. Cut phyllo sheets into strips. Place 1 tsp of spinach mixture on one end of each strip and fold into triangles. Brush with olive oil.
3. Bake for 20-25 minutes until golden brown.

10. Mediterranean Zucchini Fritters

Yield: 4 servings   **Prep Time:** 10 minutes   **Cook Time:** 10 minutes   **Cooking Method:** Pan-frying

Ingredients:
- 2 medium zucchinis, grated and squeezed dry
- 1/4 cup whole-wheat flour
- 1 egg
- 1 tbsp fresh dill, chopped
- 1 tbsp olive oil

Nutritional Information: 120 calories, 4g protein, 10g carbohydrates, 7g fat, 2g fiber, 20mg cholesterol, 120mg sodium

Directions:
1. Mix zucchini, flour, egg, and dill in a bowl. Form small patties.
2. Heat olive oil in a skillet and fry patties for 3-4 minutes per side. Serve warm.

11. Roasted Chickpeas

Yield: 4 servings   **Prep Time:** 5 minutes   **Cook Time:** 30 minutes   **Cooking Temperature:** 400°F (200°C)   **Cooking Method:** Roasting

Ingredients:
- 1 can (15 oz) chickpeas, rinsed and drained
- 1 tbsp olive oil
- 1 tsp smoked paprika

Nutritional Information: 150 calories, 6g protein, 18g carbohydrates, 5g fat, 5g fiber, 0mg cholesterol, 150mg sodium

Directions:
1. Preheat oven to 400°F (200°C). Toss chickpeas with olive oil and paprika.
2. Spread on a baking sheet and roast for 30 minutes, shaking halfway through.

12. Baba Ganoush

Yield: 4 servings   **Prep Time:** 10 minutes   **Cook Time:** 30 minutes   **Cooking Temperature:** 400°F (200°C)   **Cooking Method:** Roasting and blending

Ingredients:
- 1 large eggplant
- 1 clove garlic
- 2 tbsp tahini
- 1 tbsp lemon juice
- 1 tbsp olive oil

Nutritional Information: 100 calories, 2g protein, 8g carbohydrates, 7g fat, 3g fiber, 0mg cholesterol, 50mg sodium

Directions:
1. Preheat oven to 400°F (200°C). Roast eggplant for 30 minutes until soft. Scoop out the flesh.
2. Blend eggplant, garlic, tahini, lemon juice, and olive oil until smooth. Serve with pita bread or vegetables.

13. Grilled Vegetable Skewers

Yield: 4 servings   **Prep Time:** 10 minutes   **Cook Time:** 10 minutes   **Cooking Method:** Grilling

Ingredients:
- 1 zucchini, sliced
- 1 red bell pepper, diced
- 8 cherry tomatoes
- 1 tbsp olive oil
- 1 tsp dried oregano

Nutritional Information: 90 calories, 2g protein, 8g carbohydrates, 5g fat, 2g fiber, 0mg cholesterol, 40mg sodium

Directions:
1. Thread vegetables onto skewers. Brush with olive oil and sprinkle with oregano.
2. Grill for 2-3 minutes per side until slightly charred. Serve warm.

14. Mediterranean Deviled Eggs

Yield: 4 servings   **Prep Time:** 10 minutes   **Cook Time:** 10 minutes   **Cooking Method:** Boiling

Ingredients:
- 6 hard-boiled eggs
- 2 tbsp plain Greek yogurt
- 1 tbsp olive tapenade

Nutritional Information: 80 calories, 6g protein, 1g carbohydrates, 6g fat, 0g fiber, 190mg cholesterol, 90mg sodium

Directions:
1. Slice eggs in half and remove yolks. Mix yolks with yogurt and olive tapenade.
2. Fill egg whites with the mixture. Serve immediately.

15. Cucumber and Tomato Salad with Feta

Yield: 4 servings | **Prep Time:** 10 minutes | **Cook Time:** 0 minutes | **Cooking Method:** No-cook

Ingredients:
- 1 cucumber, diced
- 1 cup cherry tomatoes, halved
- 1/4 cup crumbled feta cheese
- 1 tbsp olive oil
- 1 tsp dried oregano

Nutritional Information: 120 calories, 4g protein, 6g carbohydrates, 9g fat, 2g fiber, 10mg cholesterol, 120mg sodium

Directions:
1. Combine cucumber, tomatoes, and feta in a bowl.
2. Drizzle with olive oil and sprinkle with oregano. Toss gently.

16. Spicy Red Lentil Dip

Yield: 4 servings | **Prep Time:** 5 minutes | **Cook Time:** 15 minutes | **Cooking Method:** Simmering and blending

Ingredients:
- 1/2 cup red lentils
- 1 clove garlic
- 1 tsp harissa paste
- 1 tbsp olive oil
- 1 tbsp lemon juice

Nutritional Information: 110 calories, 4g protein, 10g carbohydrates, 5g fat, 3g fiber, 0mg cholesterol, 80mg sodium

Directions:
1. Cook lentils in 1 cup water until soft, about 15 minutes. Drain and cool slightly.
2. Blend lentils, garlic, harissa, olive oil, and lemon juice until smooth. Serve with vegetables or crackers.

CHAPTER 6: GRAINS, PASTA, AND LEGUMES

1. Lemon Herb Farro Salad

Yield: 4 servings **Prep Time:** 10 minutes **Cook Time:** 25 minutes **Cooking Method:** Boiling

Ingredients:
- 1 cup farro
- 2 cups water or vegetable broth
- 1/2 cup cherry tomatoes, halved
- 1/4 cup chopped parsley
- 1 tbsp olive oil
- 1 tbsp lemon juice

Nutritional Information: 200 calories, 6g protein, 35g carbohydrates, 5g fat, 6g fiber, 0mg cholesterol, 150mg sodium

Directions:
1. Cook farro in water or broth for 20-25 minutes until tender. Drain and let cool slightly.
2. Mix farro with tomatoes, parsley, olive oil, and lemon juice. Serve at room temperature or chilled.

2. Chickpea and Spinach Pasta

Yield: 6 servings **Prep Time:** 10 minutes **Cook Time:** 30 minutes **Cooking Method:** Boiling and sautéing

Ingredients:
- 8 oz whole-grain pasta
- 1 can (15 oz) chickpeas, rinsed and drained
- 2 cups fresh spinach
- 2 cloves garlic, minced
- 2 tbsp olive oil

Nutritional Information: 300 calories, 12g protein, 48g carbohydrates, 7g fat, 8g fiber, 0mg cholesterol, 200mg sodium

Directions:
1. Cook pasta according to package Directions. Drain and set aside.
2. Heat olive oil in a skillet over medium heat. Sauté garlic for 1 minute, then add chickpeas and spinach. Cook until spinach wilts.
3. Toss pasta with chickpea mixture and serve.

3. Mediterranean Lentil and Quinoa Pilaf

Yield: 4 servings   **Prep Time:** 10 minutes   **Cook Time:** 25 minutes   **Cooking Method:** Simmering

Ingredients:
- 1/2 cup quinoa
- 1/2 cup green lentils
- 2 cups vegetable broth
- 1/4 cup diced onion
- 1 tbsp olive oil
- 1/2 tsp ground cumin

Nutritional Information: 220 calories, 9g protein, 35g carbohydrates, 5g fat, 7g fiber, 0mg cholesterol, 180mg sodium

Directions:

1. Heat olive oil in a pot and sauté onion for 2-3 minutes.
2. Add quinoa, lentils, broth, and cumin. Bring to a boil, then reduce heat and simmer for 20-25 minutes until liquid is absorbed.

4. Roasted Vegetable Couscous

Yield: 4 servings   **Prep Time:** 10 minutes   **Cook Time:** 15 minutes   **Cooking Temperature:** 400°F (200°C)   **Cooking Method:** Roasting

Ingredients:
- 1 cup whole-grain couscous
- 1 zucchini, diced
- 1 red bell pepper, diced
- 1 tbsp olive oil
- 1 tsp dried oregano

Nutritional Information: 210 calories, 6g protein, 38g carbohydrates, 5g fat, 4g fiber, 0mg cholesterol, 120mg sodium

Directions:

1. Preheat oven to 400°F (200°C). Toss zucchini and bell pepper with olive oil and oregano. Roast for 15 minutes.
2. Prepare couscous according to package Directions. Mix with roasted vegetables.

5. Creamy Orzo with Spinach and Feta

Yield: 4 servings   **Prep Time:** 10 minutes   **Cook Time:** 15 minutes   **Cooking Method:** Simmering

Ingredients:
- 1 cup orzo pasta
- 2 cups vegetable broth
- 1 cup fresh spinach
- 1/4 cup crumbled feta cheese
- 1 tbsp olive oil

Nutritional Information: 240 calories, 7g protein, 35g carbohydrates, 8g fat, 3g fiber, 15mg cholesterol, 180mg sodium

Directions:
1. Cook orzo in vegetable broth until tender, about 12 minutes.
2. Stir in spinach and cook for 2 more minutes. Remove from heat and mix in feta cheese and olive oil.

6. Barley and Roasted Tomato Salad

Yield: 4 servings   **Prep Time:** 10 minutes   **Cook Time:** 30 minutes   **Cooking Temperature:** 400°F (200°C)   **Cooking Method:** Boiling and roasting

Ingredients:
- 1 cup barley
- 1 cup cherry tomatoes, halved
- 1 tbsp olive oil
- 1 tbsp balsamic vinegar

Nutritional Information: 200 calories, 5g protein, 38g carbohydrates, 4g fat, 6g fiber, 0mg cholesterol, 100mg sodium

Directions:
1. Cook barley in water until tender, about 30 minutes. Drain and cool slightly.
2. Toss tomatoes with olive oil and roast at 400°F (200°C) for 15 minutes. Combine barley, tomatoes, and balsamic vinegar.

7. Spiced Lentil Stew with Brown Rice

Yield: 4 servings   **Prep Time:** 10 minutes   **Cook Time:** 30minutes   **Cooking Method:** Simmering

Ingredients:
- 1 cup green lentils
- 1/2 cup brown rice
- 4 cups vegetable broth
- 1 onion, diced
- 2 cloves garlic, minced
- 1 tsp ground cumin
- 1 tbsp olive oil

Nutritional Information: 280 calories, 10g protein, 46g carbohydrates, 6g fat, 8g fiber, 0mg cholesterol, 150mg sodium

Directions:
1. Heat olive oil in a pot and sauté onion and garlic for 2-3 minutes.
2. Add lentils, rice, broth, and cumin. Simmer for 30 minutes until lentils and rice are tender.

8. Mediterranean Chickpea and Bulgur Salad

Yield: 4 servings   **Prep Time:** 10 minutes   **Cook Time:** 10 minutes   **Cooking Method:** Boiling

Ingredients:
- 1 cup bulgur wheat
- 1 can (15 oz) chickpeas, rinsed and drained
- 1/2 cup cherry tomatoes, halved
- 1 tbsp olive oil
- 1 tbsp lemon juice

Nutritional Information: 250 calories, 8g protein, 40g carbohydrates, 7g fat, 5g fiber, 0mg cholesterol, 140mg sodium

Directions:
1. Cook bulgur according to package Directions. Let cool slightly.
2. Combine bulgur, chickpeas, tomatoes, olive oil, and lemon juice in a bowl. Toss well and serve.

9. Pasta Primavera with Fresh Vegetables

Yield: 4 servings   **Prep Time:** 10 minutes   **Cook Time:** 15 minutes   **Cooking Method:** Boiling and sautéing

Ingredients:

- 8 oz whole-grain spaghetti
- 1 cup broccoli florets
- 1 zucchini, sliced
- 1/2 cup cherry tomatoes, halved
- 2 tbsp olive oil
- 1 clove garlic, minced

Nutritional Information: 300 calories, 10g protein, 50g carbohydrates, 7g fat, 6g fiber, 0mg cholesterol, 150mg sodium

Directions:

1. Cook spaghetti according to package Directions. Reserve 1/2 cup pasta water.
2. Heat olive oil in a skillet. Sauté garlic, broccoli, and zucchini for 5 minutes. Add tomatoes and pasta water. Toss with spaghetti and serve.

10. Quinoa and Black Bean Bowl

Yield: 4 servings   **Prep Time:** 10 minutes   **Cook Time:** 15 minutes   **Cooking Method:** Boiling

Ingredients:

- 1 cup quinoa
- 1 can (15 oz) black beans, rinsed and drained
- 1/2 cup diced red bell pepper
- 2 tbsp olive oil
- 1 tbsp lime juice

Nutritional Information: 260 calories, 9g protein, 40g carbohydrates, 8g fat, 6g fiber, 0mg cholesterol, 140mg sodium

Directions:

1. Cook quinoa according to package Directions. Let cool slightly.
2. Combine quinoa, black beans, bell pepper, olive oil, and lime juice in a bowl. Toss well.

11. Roasted Chickpeas and Freekeh Salad

Yield: 4 servings **Prep Time:** 10 minutes **Cook Time:** 30 minutes **Cooking Method:** Boiling and roasting

Ingredients:
- 1 cup cooked freekeh
- 1 can (15 oz) chickpeas, rinsed and drained
- 1 tbsp olive oil
- 1 tsp smoked paprika
- 1/4 cup chopped parsley

Nutritional Information: 230 calories, 8g protein, 36g carbohydrates, 5g fat, 6g fiber, 0mg cholesterol, 120mg sodium

Directions:
1. Roast chickpeas with olive oil and paprika at 400°F (200°C) for 20 minutes.
2. Combine freekeh, chickpeas, and parsley in a bowl. Serve warm or chilled.

12. Tomato and Barley Risotto

Yield: 4 servings **Prep Time:** 10 minutes **Cook Time:** 40 minutes **Cooking Method:** Simmering

Ingredients:
- 1 cup pearl barley
- 3 cups vegetable broth
- 1 cup diced tomatoes
- 1 onion, diced
- 2 tbsp olive oil

Nutritional Information: 250 calories, 6g protein, 45g carbohydrates, 6g fat, 7g fiber, 0mg cholesterol, 150mg sodium

Directions:
1. Heat olive oil in a pot and sauté onion for 3 minutes. Add barley and cook for 1 minute.
2. Gradually add broth and tomatoes, stirring frequently, until barley is tender (about 40 minutes).

13. Whole-Wheat Pasta with Lentil Sauce

Yield: 4 servings   **Prep Time:** 10 minutes   **Cook Time:** 30 minutes   **Cooking Method:** Boiling and simmering

Ingredients:
- 8 oz whole-wheat pasta
- 1 cup cooked lentils
- 1 can (15 oz) diced tomatoes
- 1 tbsp olive oil
- 1 clove garlic, minced

Nutritional Information: 280 calories, 12g protein, 45g carbohydrates, 6g fat, 7g fiber, 0mg cholesterol, 200mg sodium

Directions:
1. Cook pasta according to package Directions.
2. Heat olive oil in a pot and sauté garlic. Add lentils and tomatoes. Simmer for 15 minutes. Toss with pasta and serve.

14. Farro and Roasted Red Pepper Salad

Yield: 4 servings   **Prep Time:** 10 minutes   **Cook Time:** 25 minutes   **Cooking Method:** Boiling and roasting

Ingredients:
- 1 cup farro
- 1/2 cup roasted red peppers, diced
- 1 tbsp olive oil
- 1 tbsp balsamic vinegar

Nutritional Information: 200 calories, 6g protein, 36g carbohydrates, 5g fat, 5g fiber, 0mg cholesterol, 120mg sodium

Directions:
1. Cook farro according to package Directions. Let cool.
2. Mix farro, roasted red peppers, olive oil, and balsamic vinegar in a bowl. Serve chilled.

15. Bulgur Wheat and Lentil Pilaf

Yield: 4 servings **Prep Time:** 10 minutes **Cook Time:** 25 minutes **Cooking Method:** Simmering

Ingredients:

- 1 cup cooked freekeh
- 1 can (15 oz) chickpeas, rinsed and drained
- 1 tbsp olive oil
- 1 tsp smoked paprika
- 1/4 cup chopped parsley

Nutritional Information: 220 calories, 8g protein, 35g carbohydrates, 6g fat, 7g fiber, 0mg cholesterol, 140mg sodium

Directions:

1. Heat olive oil in a pot and sauté onion for 3 minutes.
2. Add bulgur, lentils, and broth. Simmer for 20 minutes or until liquid is absorbed.

16. Warm Lentil and Couscous Salad

Yield: 4 servings **Prep Time:** 10 minutes **Cook Time:** 15 minutes **Cooking Method:** Boiling

Ingredients:

- 1 cup cooked couscous
- 1/2 cup cooked lentils
- 1/4 cup diced cucumber
- 1 tbsp olive oil
- 1 tbsp lemon juice

Nutritional Information: 190 calories, 6g protein, 30g carbohydrates, 5g fat, 4g fiber, 0mg cholesterol, 120mg sodium

Directions:

1. Mix couscous, lentils, and cucumber in a bowl.
2. Drizzle with olive oil and lemon juice. Toss well and serve.

CHAPTER 7: SEAFOOD DELIGHTS

1. Lemon Garlic Shrimp Skillet

Yield: 4 servings   **Prep Time:** 10 minutes   **Cook Time:** 10 minutes   **Cooking Method:** Sautéing

Ingredients:
- 1 lb shrimp, peeled and deveined
- 2 tbsp olive oil
- 2 cloves garlic, minced
- 1 tbsp lemon juice
- 1/4 tsp red pepper flakes

Nutritional Information: 180 calories, 22g protein, 1g carbohydrates, 9g fat, 0g fiber, 190mg cholesterol, 300mg sodium

Directions:
1. Heat olive oil in a skillet over medium heat. Add garlic and cook for 1 minute.
2. Add shrimp and red pepper flakes. Sauté for 4-5 minutes or until shrimp are pink.
3. Stir in lemon juice and serve warm.

2. Grilled Salmon with Herbs

Yield: 4 servings   **Prep Time:** 10 minutes   **Cook Time:** 10 minutes   **Cooking Method:** Grilling

Ingredients:
- 4 salmon fillets (6 oz each)
- 2 tbsp olive oil
- 1 tbsp fresh dill, chopped
- 1 tbsp lemon juice

Nutritional Information: 280 calories, 25g protein, 0g carbohydrates, 20g fat, 0g fiber, 60mg cholesterol, 150mg sodium

Directions:
1. Brush salmon with olive oil, dill, and lemon juice.
2. Grill over medium-high heat for 4-5 minutes per side. Serve immediately.

3. Baked Cod with Tomatoes and Olives

Yield: 4 servings   **Prep Time:** 10 minutes   **Cook Time:** 20 minutes   **Cooking Temperature:** 375°F (190°C)   **Cooking Method:** Baking

Ingredients:
- 4 cod fillets (6 oz each)
- 1 cup cherry tomatoes, halved
- 1/4 cup Kalamata olives, sliced
- 2 tbsp olive oil

Nutritional Information: 210 calories, 30g protein, 3g carbohydrates, 7g fat, 1g fiber, 55mg cholesterol, 200mg sodium

Directions:
1. Preheat oven to 375°F (190°C). Arrange cod, tomatoes, and olives in a baking dish.
2. Drizzle with olive oil and bake for 20 minutes or until fish flakes easily.

4. Shrimp and Zucchini Noodles

Yield: 4 servings   **Prep Time:** 15 minutes   **Cook Time:** 10 minutes   **Cooking Method:** Sautéing

Ingredients:
- 1 lb shrimp, peeled and deveined
- 2 medium zucchinis, spiralized
- 2 tbsp olive oil
- 1 clove garlic, minced
- 1 tbsp lemon juice

Nutritional Information: 200 calories, 20g protein, 4g carbohydrates, 10g fat, 2g fiber, 190mg cholesterol, 150mg sodium

Directions:
1. Heat olive oil in a skillet. Add garlic and shrimp, cooking for 4-5 minutes.
2. Toss in zucchini noodles and cook for 2 minutes. Stir in lemon juice and serve.

5. Sardines in Olive Oil with Lemon

Yield: 2 servings   **Prep Time:** 5 minutes   **Cook Time:** 0 minutes   **Cooking Method:** No-cook

Ingredients:
- 1 can (4 oz) sardines in olive oil
- 1 tbsp lemon juice
- 1 tbsp chopped parsley

Nutritional Information: 140 calories, 14g protein, 0g carbohydrates, 10g fat, 0g fiber, 30mg cholesterol, 120mg sodium

Directions:
1. Drain sardines and arrange on a plate.
2. Drizzle with lemon juice and sprinkle with parsley. Serve with whole-grain bread.

6. Grilled Tuna Steaks with Capers

Yield: 4 servings   **Prep Time:** 10 minutes   **Cook Time:** 10 minutes   **Cooking Method:** Grilling

Ingredients:
- 4 tuna steaks (6 oz each)
- 2 tbsp olive oil
- 1 tbsp capers
- 1 tbsp lemon juice

Nutritional Information: 260 calories, 34g protein, 0g carbohydrates, 12g fat, 0g fiber, 70mg cholesterol, 150mg sodium

Directions:
1. Brush tuna steaks with olive oil and grill for 3-4 minutes per side.
2. Drizzle with lemon juice and top with capers. Serve warm.

7. Mediterranean Mussels in White Wine Sauce

Yield: 2 servings | **Prep Time:** 10 minutes | **Cook Time:** 10 minutes | **Cooking Method:** Simmering

Ingredients:
- 2 lbs fresh mussels, cleaned
- 1/2 cup white wine
- 1 clove garlic, minced
- 2 tbsp olive oil
- 1 tbsp parsley, chopped

Nutritional Information: 200 calories, 18g protein, 4g carbohydrates, 7g fat, 0g fiber, 45mg cholesterol, 300mg sodium

Directions:
1. Heat olive oil in a large pot. Add garlic and cook for 1 minute.
2. Add mussels with paprika to your taste and wine. Cover and steam for 5-7 minutes until mussels open. Sprinkle with parsley.

8. Roasted Salmon with Asparagus

Yield: 4 servings | **Prep Time:** 10 minutes | **Cook Time:** 15 minutes | **Cooking Temperature:** 400°F (200°C) | **Cooking Method:** Roasting

Ingredients:
- 4 salmon fillets (6 oz each)
- 1 bunch asparagus, trimmed
- 2 tbsp olive oil
- 1 tsp garlic powder

Nutritional Information: 290 calories, 28g protein, 2g carbohydrates, 20g fat, 1g fiber, 60mg cholesterol, 120mg sodium

Directions:
1. Preheat oven to 400°F (200°C). Arrange salmon and asparagus on a baking tray.
2. Drizzle with olive oil and sprinkle with garlic powder. Roast for 15 minutes.

9. Shrimp and Farro Salad

Yield: 2 servings   **Prep Time:** 10 minutes   **Cook Time:** 15 minutes   **Cooking Method:** Boiling and mixing

Ingredients:
- 1 cup cooked farro
- 8 oz shrimp, peeled and deveined
- 1 cup cherry tomatoes, halved
- 2 tbsp olive oil
- 1 tbsp lemon juice

Nutritional Information: 250 calories, 18g protein, 22g carbohydrates, 8g fat, 3g fiber, 90mg cholesterol, 180mg sodium

Directions:
1. Boil shrimp for 2-3 minutes until pink. Drain and cool slightly.
2. Toss shrimp with farro, tomatoes, olive oil, and lemon juice. Serve chilled or at room temperature.

10. Grilled Prawns with Garlic and Lemon

Yield: 4 servings   **Prep Time:** 10 minutes   **Cook Time:** 8 minutes   **Cooking Method:** Grilling

Ingredients:
- 1 lb large prawns, shell-on
- 3 tbsp olive oil
- 2 cloves garlic, minced
- 1 tbsp lemon juice

Nutritional Information: 210 calories, 23g protein, 0g carbohydrates, 13g fat, 0g fiber, 190mg cholesterol, 150mg sodium

Directions:
1. Toss prawns with olive oil, garlic, and lemon juice.
2. Grill over medium heat for 3-4 minutes per side or until pink and cooked through. Serve immediately.

11. Baked Sea Bass with Lemon and Thyme

Yield: 4 servings   **Prep Time:** 10 minutes   **Cook Time:** 20 minutes   **Cooking Temperature:** 375°F (190°C)   **Cooking Method:** Baking

Ingredients:
- 4 sea bass fillets (6 oz each)
- 2 tbsp olive oil
- 2 tbsp lemon juice
- 1 tsp dried thyme

Nutritional Information: 200 calories, 32g protein, 0g carbohydrates, 8g fat, 0g fiber, 65mg cholesterol, 120mg sodium

Directions:
1. Preheat oven to 375°F (190°C). Arrange sea bass fillets in a baking dish.
2. Drizzle with olive oil and lemon juice, and sprinkle thyme over the top.
3. Bake for 20 minutes or until the fish flakes easily with a fork.

12. Mediterranean Clam Pasta

Yield: 4 servings   **Prep Time:** 10 minutes   **Cook Time:** 15 minutes   **Cooking Method:** Boiling and sautéing

Ingredients:
- 1 lb clams, cleaned
- 8 oz whole-grain spaghetti
- 3 tbsp olive oil
- 2 cloves garlic, minced
- 1/4 cup white wine

Nutritional Information: 320 calories, 18g protein, 45g carbohydrates, 8g fat, 4g fiber, 45mg cholesterol, 180mg sodium

Directions:
1. Cook spaghetti according to package Directions.
2. Heat olive oil in a skillet, add garlic, and cook for 1 minute. Add clams and white wine, cover, and steam for 5 minutes until clams open.
3. Toss spaghetti with clam mixture and serve.

13. Sardine and Avocado Toast

Yield: 2 servings   **Prep Time:** 5 minutes   **Cook Time:** 0 minutes   **Cooking Method:** No-cook

Ingredients:
- 2 slices whole-grain bread
- 1 avocado, mashed
- 1 can (4 oz) sardines in olive oil, drained
- 1 tbsp lemon juice

Nutritional Information: 250 calories, 12g protein, 16g carbohydrates, 16g fat, 5g fiber, 30mg cholesterol, 200mg sodium

Directions:
1. Spread mashed avocado on toasted bread.
2. Top with sardines and drizzle with lemon juice. Serve immediately.

14. Grilled Octopus with Olive Oil and Lemon

Yield: 4 servings   **Prep Time:** 10 minutes   **Cook Time:** 30 minutes   **Cooking Method:** Boiling and grilling

Ingredients:
- 1 lb octopus, cleaned
- 3 tbsp olive oil
- 1 tbsp lemon juice
- 1 tsp dried oregano

Nutritional Information: 180 calories, 20g protein, 1g carbohydrates, 10g fat, 0g fiber, 80mg cholesterol, 300mg sodium

Directions:
1. Boil octopus in salted water for 20 minutes. Drain and cool slightly.
2. Brush with olive oil and grill for 5-7 minutes until lightly charred. Drizzle with lemon juice and sprinkle oregano before serving.

15. Baked Scallops with Garlic and Parmesan

Yield: 4 servings   **Prep Time:** 10 minutes   **Cook Time:** 15 minutes   **Cooking Temperature:** 400°F (200°C)   **Cooking Method:** Roasting

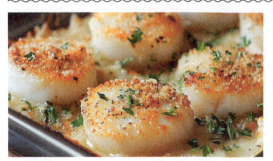

Ingredients:
- 1 lb scallops
- 2 tbsp olive oil
- 2 cloves garlic, minced
- 2 tbsp grated Parmesan cheese

Nutritional Information: 220 calories, 23g protein, 1g carbohydrates, 14g fat, 0g fiber, 60mg cholesterol, 180mg sodium

Directions:
1. Preheat oven to 400°F (200°C). Arrange scallops in a baking dish.
2. Drizzle with olive oil, sprinkle garlic and Parmesan on top. Bake for 15 minutes or until golden and cooked through.

16. Steamed Fish with Lemon and Capers

Yield: 4 servings   **Prep Time:** 10 minutes   **Cook Time:** 10 minutes   **Cooking Method:** Steaming

Ingredients:
- 4 white fish fillets (6 oz each, e.g., cod or haddock)
- 2 tbsp olive oil
- 1 tbsp capers
- 1 tbsp lemon juice

Nutritional Information: 190 calories, 30g protein, 0g carbohydrates, 8g fat, 0g fiber, 50mg cholesterol, 120mg sodium

Directions:
1. Place fish in a steamer basket over boiling water. Cover and steam for 8-10 minutes or until cooked through.
2. Drizzle with olive oil and lemon juice, and top with capers before serving.

CHAPTER 8: VEGETARIAN FAVORITES

1. Ratatouille with Lentils

Yield: 4 servings   **Prep Time:** 10 minutes   **Cook Time:** 30 minutes   **Cooking Method:** Simmering

Ingredients:
- 1 zucchini, diced
- 1 eggplant, diced
- 1 red bell pepper, diced
- 1 cup cooked lentils
- 2 cups diced tomatoes
- 2 tbsp olive oil
- 1 tsp dried thyme

Nutritional Information: 210 calories, 8g protein, 24g carbohydrates, 8g fat, 6g fiber, 0mg cholesterol, 200mg sodium

Directions:
1. Heat olive oil in a large skillet over medium heat. Sauté zucchini, eggplant, and bell pepper for 5 minutes.
2. Add lentils, tomatoes, and thyme. Simmer for 25 minutes, stirring occasionally. Serve warm.

2. Spinach and Feta Stuffed Peppers

Yield: 4 servings **Prep Time:** 15 minutes **Cook Time:** 30 minutes **Cooking Temperature:** 375°F (190°C) **Cooking Method:** Baking

Ingredients:
- 4 bell peppers, halved and seeds removed
- 2 cups fresh spinach, chopped
- 1/2 cup crumbled feta cheese
- 1 tbsp olive oil

Nutritional Information: 190 calories, 6g protein, 10g carbohydrates, 12g fat, 3g fiber, 15mg cholesterol, 150mg sodium

Directions:
1. Preheat oven to 375°F (190°C). Sauté spinach in olive oil until wilted.
2. Mix spinach with feta and stuff into bell peppers. Bake for 30 minutes.

3. Zucchini Noodle Pesto Salad

Yield: 2 servings   **Prep Time:** 10 minutes   **Cook Time:** 0 minutes   **Cooking Method:** No-cook

Ingredients:
- 2 zucchinis, spiralized
- 2 tbsp pesto
- 1/2 cup cherry tomatoes, halved
- 1 tbsp pine nuts

Nutritional Information: 170 calories, 4g protein, 10g carbohydrates, 13g fat, 2g fiber, 5mg cholesterol, 50mg sodium

Directions:
1. Toss zucchini noodles with pesto in a large bowl.
2. Top with cherry tomatoes and pine nuts. Serve chilled.

4. Grilled Vegetable Platter with Hummus

Yield: 4 servings   **Prep Time:** 10 minutes   **Cook Time:** 15 minutes   **Cooking Method:** Grilling

Ingredients:
- 1 zucchini, sliced
- 1 eggplant, sliced
- 1 red bell pepper, quartered
- 1 tbsp olive oil
- 1/2 cup hummus

Nutritional Information: 220 calories, 6g protein, 16g carbohydrates, 12g fat, 4g fiber, 0mg cholesterol, 120mg sodium

Directions:
1. Brush vegetables with olive oil and grill for 3-4 minutes per side.
2. Arrange on a platter and serve with hummus.

5. Mediterranean Lentil Soup

Yield: 2 servings   **Prep Time:** 10 minutes   **Cook Time:** 30 minutes   **Cooking Method:** Simmering

Ingredients:
- 1 cup lentils
- 4 cups vegetable broth
- 1 cup diced carrots
- 1 onion, diced
- 2 tbsp olive oil
- 1 tsp ground cumin

Nutritional Information: 200 calories, 8g protein, 25g carbohydrates, 6g fat, 6g fiber, 0mg cholesterol, 250mg sodium

Directions:
1. Heat olive oil in a pot over medium heat. Sauté carrots and onion for 5 minutes.
2. Add lentils, broth, and cumin. Simmer for 25 minutes or until lentils are tender.

6. Mediterranean Chickpea Salad

Yield: 4 servings   **Prep Time:** 10 minutes   **Cook Time:** 0 minutes   **Cooking Method:** No-cook

Ingredients:
- 1 can (15 oz) chickpeas, rinsed and drained
- 1/2 cup cherry tomatoes, halved
- 1/4 cup diced cucumber
- 2 tbsp olive oil
- 1 tbsp lemon juice

Nutritional Information: 180 calories, 6g protein, 20g carbohydrates, 8g fat, 5g fiber, 0mg cholesterol, 180mg sodium

Directions:
1. Combine chickpeas, tomatoes, cucumber, olive oil, and lemon juice in a bowl. Toss gently. Serve immediately.

7. Eggplant and Tomato Stew

Yield: 2 servings   **Prep Time:** 10 minutes   **Cook Time:** 25 minutes   **Cooking Method:** Simmering

Ingredients:

- 1 eggplant, diced
- 2 cups diced tomatoes
- 1 onion, diced
- 2 tbsp olive oil
- 1 tsp dried oregano

Nutritional Information: 150 calories, 3g protein, 14g carbohydrates, 9g fat, 5g fiber, 0mg cholesterol, 200mg sodium

Directions:

1. Heat olive oil in a pot over medium heat. Sauté eggplant and onion for 5 minutes.
2. Add tomatoes and oregano. Simmer for 20 minutes. Serve warm.

8. Spinach and Ricotta Frittata

Yield: 4 servings   **Prep Time:** 10 minutes   **Cook Time:** 20 minutes   **Cooking Temperature:** 375°F (190°C)   **Cooking Method:** Baking

Ingredients:

- 6 large eggs
- 1 cup spinach, chopped
- 1/2 cup ricotta cheese
- 1 tbsp olive oil

Nutritional Information: 190 calories, 12g protein, 2g carbohydrates, 14g fat, 1g fiber, 220mg cholesterol, 150mg sodium

Directions:

1. Preheat oven to 375°F (190°C). Whisk eggs in a bowl. Mix in spinach and ricotta.
2. Heat olive oil in an ovenproof skillet. Pour in egg mixture. Bake for 20 minutes.

9. Roasted Cauliflower and Tahini Bowl

Yield: 4 servings **Prep Time:** 10 minutes **Cook Time:** 25 minutes **Cooking Temperature:** 400°F (200°C) **Cooking Method:** Roasting

Ingredients:

- 1 head cauliflower, cut into florets
- 2 tbsp olive oil
- 1 tsp smoked paprika
- 2 tbsp tahini
- 1 tbsp lemon juice

Nutritional Information: 190 calories, 4g protein, 12g carbohydrates, 12g fat, 4g fiber, 0mg cholesterol, 100mg sodium

Directions:

1. Preheat oven to 400°F (200°C). Toss cauliflower florets with olive oil and paprika.
2. Roast for 25 minutes or until tender. Drizzle with tahini and lemon juice before serving.

10. Stuffed Zucchini Boats

Yield: 4 servings **Prep Time:** 15 minutes **Cook Time:** 25 minutes **Cooking Temperature:** 375°F (190°C) **Cooking Method:** Baking

Ingredients:

- 6 large eggs
- 4 medium zucchinis, halved and hollowed
- 1 cup cooked quinoa
- 1/2 cup diced tomatoes
- 1/4 cup crumbled feta cheese
- 1 tbsp olive oil

Nutritional Information: 210 calories, 6g protein, 22g carbohydrates, 8g fat, 3g fiber, 10mg cholesterol, 150mg sodium

Directions:

1. Preheat oven to 375°F (190°C). Arrange zucchini halves in a baking dish.
2. Mix quinoa, tomatoes, and feta. Stuff into zucchini halves. Drizzle with olive oil and bake for 25 minutes.

11. Sweet Potato and Chickpea Bowl

Yield: 4 servings   **Prep Time:** 10 minutes   **Cook Time:** 30 minutes   **Cooking Temperature:** 400°F (200°C)   **Cooking Method:** Roasting

Ingredients:
- 2 medium sweet potatoes, diced
- 1 can (15 oz) chickpeas, rinsed and drained
- 2 tbsp olive oil
- 1 tsp ground cumin

Nutritional Information: 230 calories, 5g protein, 32g carbohydrates, 8g fat, 6g fiber, 0mg cholesterol, 120mg sodium

Directions:
1. Preheat oven to 400°F (200°C). Toss sweet potatoes and chickpeas with olive oil and cumin.
2. Spread on a baking sheet and roast for 30 minutes. Serve warm.

12. Mediterranean Stuffed Eggplant

Yield: 4 servings   **Prep Time:** 15 minutes   **Cook Time:** 30 minutes   **Cooking Temperature:** 375°F (190°C)   **Cooking Method:** Baking

Ingredients:
- 2 large eggplants, halved and hollowed
- 1 cup diced tomatoes
- 1/2 cup cooked lentils
- 1/4 cup crumbled feta cheese
- 1 tbsp olive oil

Nutritional Information: 200 calories, 7g protein, 20g carbohydrates, 8g fat, 5g fiber, 10mg cholesterol, 150mg sodium

Directions:
1. Preheat oven to 375°F (190°C). Arrange eggplant halves in a baking dish.
2. Mix tomatoes, lentils, and feta. Stuff into eggplant halves. Drizzle with olive oil and bake for 30 minutes.

13. Greek Lentil Salad

Yield: 2 servings   **Prep Time:** 10 minutes   **Cook Time:** 15 minutes   **Cooking Method:** Boiling

Ingredients:
- 1 cup cooked lentils
- 1/2 cup diced cucumber and onion
- 1/2 cup cherry tomatoes, halved
- 2 tbsp olive oil
- 1 tbsp red wine vinegar

Nutritional Information: 190 calories, 6g protein, 20g carbohydrates, 8g fat, 4g fiber, 0mg cholesterol, 150mg sodium

Directions:
1. Cook lentils according to package Directions and let cool slightly.
2. Toss lentils with cucumber, onion, tomatoes, olive oil, and vinegar. Serve chilled.

14. Mediterranean Spinach Pie (Spanakopita)

Yield: 6 servings   **Prep Time:** 20 minutes   **Cook Time:** 30 minutes   **Cooking Temperature:** 375°F (190°C)   **Cooking Method:** Baking

Ingredients:
- 1 cup fresh spinach, chopped
- 1/2 cup crumbled feta cheese
- 6 sheets phyllo dough
- 2 tbsp olive oil

Nutritional Information: 190 calories, 6g protein, 15g carbohydrates, 10g fat, 1g fiber, 15mg cholesterol, 200mg sodium

Directions:
1. Preheat oven to 375°F (190°C). Mix spinach and feta in a bowl.
2. Layer phyllo sheets, brushing each with olive oil. Add filling and fold into triangles.
3. Bake for 25-30 minutes or until golden brown.

CHAPTER 9: SWEET TREATS AND DESSERTS

1. Greek Yogurt and Honey Parfait

Yield: 4 servings   **Prep Time:** 5 minutes   **Cook Time:** 0 minutes   **Cooking Method:** Assembly

Ingredients:
- 2 cups plain Greek yogurt
- 2 tbsp honey
- 1/4 cup granola
- 1/4 cup fresh berries

Nutritional Information: 190 calories, 10g protein, 22g carbohydrates, 5g fat, 2g fiber, 10mg cholesterol, 55mg sodium

Directions:
1. In a glass or bowl, layer Greek yogurt, honey, granola, and berries.
2. Repeat layers and serve immediately.

2. Olive Oil and Orange Cake

Yield: 6 servings   **Prep Time:** 10 minutes   **Cook Time:** 35 minutes   **Cooking Temperature:** 375°F (190°C)   **Cooking Method:** Baking

Ingredients:
- 1/2 cup olive oil
- 1/2 cup honey
- 2 large eggs
- 1/2 cup orange juice
- 1 1/2 cups whole-wheat flour
- 1 tsp baking powder

Nutritional Information: 220 calories, 4g protein, 26g carbohydrates, 12g fat, 2g fiber, 30mg cholesterol, 80mg sodium

Directions:
1. Preheat oven to 350°F (175°C). Mix olive oil, honey, eggs, and orange juice in a bowl.
2. Add flour and baking powder, stirring until smooth. Pour into a greased 8-inch pan.
3. Bake for 35 minutes or until a toothpick comes out clean.

3. Baked Pears with Walnuts and Honey

Yield: 4 servings   **Prep Time:** 5 minutes   **Cook Time:** 20 minutes   **Cooking Temperature:** 375°F (190°C)   **Cooking Method:** Baking

Ingredients:
- 4 medium pears, halved and cored
- 2 tbsp honey
- 1/4 cup chopped walnuts
- 1/2 tsp cinnamon

Nutritional Information: 180 calories, 2g protein, 30g carbohydrates, 7g fat, 4g fiber, 0mg cholesterol, 10mg sodium

Directions:
1. Preheat oven to 375°F (190°C). Arrange pears in a baking dish.
2. Drizzle with honey, sprinkle with walnuts and cinnamon. Bake for 20 minutes.

4. Dark Chocolate and Almond Clusters

Yield: 6 servings   **Prep Time:** 5 minutes   **Cook Time:** 5 minutes   **Cooking Method:** Melting

Ingredients:
- 1 cup dark chocolate chips
- 1/2 cup whole almonds

Nutritional Information: 170 calories, 3g protein, 14g carbohydrates, 11g fat, 3g fiber, 0mg cholesterol, 5mg sodium

Directions:
1. Melt dark chocolate in a microwave or double boiler. Stir in almonds.
2. Drop spoonfuls onto parchment paper and refrigerate until set.

5. Fresh Fruit Salad with Mint

Yield: 2 servings   **Prep Time:** 10 minutes   **Cook Time:** 0 minutes   **Cooking Method:** No-cook

Ingredients:
- 1 cup diced watermelon
- 1 cup diced cantaloupe
- 1 cup blueberries
- 1 tbsp fresh mint, chopped

Nutritional Information: 100 calories, 1g protein, 25g carbohydrates, 0g fat, 3g fiber, 0mg cholesterol, 10mg sodium

Directions:
1. Combine all fruit in a large bowl. Sprinkle with mint and toss gently. Serve immediately.

6. Lemon and Yogurt Bars

Yield: 6 servings   **Prep Time:** 10 minutes   **Cook Time:** 25 minutes   **Cooking Temperature:** 375°F (190°C)   **Cooking Method:** Baking

Ingredients:
- 1 cup Greek yogurt
- 1/4 cup honey
- 1 egg
- 1/2 cup almond flour
- 1 tbsp lemon zest

Nutritional Information: 150 calories, 6g protein, 16g carbohydrates, 7g fat, 2g fiber, 30mg cholesterol, 20mg sodium

Directions:
1. Preheat oven to 350°F (175°C). Mix all ingredients in a bowl until smooth.
2. Pour into a greased baking dish and bake for 25 minutes. Cool before cutting.

7. Roasted Figs with Honey and Almonds

Yield: 6 servings **Prep Time:** 5 minutes **Cook Time:** 15 minutes **Cooking Temperature:** 375°F (190°C) **Cooking Method:** Roasting

Ingredients:
- 8 fresh figs, halved
- 2 tbsp honey
- 1/4 cup sliced almonds

Nutritional Information: 160 calories, 2g protein, 25g carbohydrates, 7g fat, 3g fiber, 0mg cholesterol, 5mg sodium

Directions:
1. Preheat oven to 375°F (190°C). Arrange figs on a baking sheet.
2. Drizzle with honey and sprinkle with almonds. Roast for 15 minutes.

8. Apple and Oat Crumble

Yield: 6 servings **Prep Time:** 10 minutes **Cook Time:** 25 minutes **Cooking Temperature:** 375°F (190°C) **Cooking Method:** Baking

Ingredients:
- 2 apples, sliced
- 1/2 cup rolled oats
- 2 tbsp olive oil
- 2 tbsp honey
- 1/2 tsp cinnamon

Nutritional Information: 180 calories, 2g protein, 32g carbohydrates, 6g fat, 4g fiber, 0mg cholesterol, 5mg sodium

Directions:
1. Preheat oven to 375°F (190°C). Arrange apples in a baking dish.
2. Mix oats, olive oil, honey, and cinnamon. Sprinkle over apples. Bake for 25 minutes.

9. Orange and Almond Flourless Cake

Yield: 6 servings   **Prep Time:** 15minutes   **Cook Time:** 40 minutes   **Cooking Temperature:** 375°F (190°C)   **Cooking Method:** Baking

Ingredients:

- 2 large oranges
- 1 1/2 cups almond flour
- 3 large eggs
- 1/4 cup honey
- 1 tsp baking powder

Nutritional Information: 230 calories, 8g protein, 21g carbohydrates, 13g fat, 3g fiber, 55mg cholesterol, 50mg sodium

Directions:

1. Preheat oven to 350°F (175°C). Boil oranges for 20 minutes, then puree in a blender.
2. In a bowl, mix orange puree, almond flour, eggs, honey, and baking powder.
3. Pour into a greased pan and bake for 40 minutes. Cool before serving.

10. Greek Baklava Bites

Yield: 6 servings   **Prep Time:** 15 minutes   **Cook Time:** 20 minutes   **Cooking Temperature:** 375°F (190°C)   **Cooking Method:** Baking

Ingredients:

- 6 sheets phyllo dough
- 1/2 cup chopped walnuts
- 1/4 cup honey
- 1 tsp cinnamon

Nutritional Information: 190 calories, 3g protein, 25g carbohydrates, 9g fat, 2g fiber, 0mg cholesterol, 50mg sodium

Directions:

1. Preheat oven to 375°F (190°C). Layer phyllo sheets, brushing each with honey.
2. Sprinkle with walnuts and cinnamon, then roll tightly and cut into bite-sized pieces.
3. Bake for 20 minutes until golden brown.

11. Dark Chocolate Dipped Strawberries

Yield: 4 servings　　**Prep Time:** 10 minutes　　**Cook Time:** 0 minutes　　**Cooking Method:** No-cook

Ingredients:
- 1/2 cup dark chocolate chips
- 16 large strawberries

Nutritional Information: 110 calories, 1g protein, 15g carbohydrates, 6g fat, 2g fiber, 0mg cholesterol, 5mg sodium

Directions:
1. Melt chocolate chips in a microwave or double boiler.
2. Dip strawberries into melted chocolate and place on parchment paper. Let cool and set.

12. Honey and Yogurt Panna Cotta

Yield: 2 servings　　**Prep Time:** 10 minutes　　**Cook Time:** 10 minutes (plus chilling time)　　**Cooking Method:** Simmering

Ingredients:
- 1 cup plain Greek yogurt
- 1/2 cup milk
- 2 tbsp honey
- 1 tsp vanilla extract
- 1 packet unflavored gelatin

Nutritional Information: 150 calories, 9g protein, 16g carbohydrates, 4g fat, 1g fiber, 10mg cholesterol, 50mg sodium

Directions:
1. Heat milk, honey, and vanilla in a saucepan until warm (do not boil). Stir in gelatin until dissolved.
2. Mix with Greek yogurt and pour into molds. Chill in the refrigerator for 4 hours or until set, add berries to your taste

CHAPTER 10: BEVERAGES AND CONDIMENTS

1. Lemon Mint Cooler

Yield: 4 servings   **Prep Time:** 5 minutes   **Cook Time:** 0 minutes   **Cooking Method:** Blending

Ingredients:
- 2 cups cold water
- 1/4 cup freshly squeezed lemon juice
- 1 tbsp honey
- 6 fresh mint leaves
- Ice cubes

Nutritional Information: 30 calories, 0g protein, 8g carbohydrates, 0g fat, 0g fiber, 0mg cholesterol, 5mg sodium

Directions:
1. Combine water, lemon juice, honey, and mint leaves in a blender. Blend for 30 seconds.
2. Strain if desired and serve over ice.

2. Mediterranean Herb Vinaigrette

Yield: 6 servings   **Prep Time:** 5 minutes   **Cook Time:** 0 minutes   **Cooking Method:** Mixing

Ingredients:
- 1/4 cup extra virgin olive oil
- 2 tbsp red wine vinegar
- 1 clove garlic, minced
- 1 tsp dried oregano
- 1/2 tsp Dijon mustard

Nutritional Information: 80 calories, 0g protein, 0g carbohydrates, 9g fat, 0g fiber, 0mg cholesterol, 5mg sodium

Directions:
1. Combine all ingredients in a small jar. Shake well to mix.
2. Serve immediately or refrigerate for up to one week.

3. Cucumber and Basil Infused Water

Yield: 4 servings   **Prep Time:** 5 minutes   **Cook Time:** 0 minutes   **Cooking Method:** Infusion

Ingredients:
- 4 cups cold water
- 1 cucumber, thinly sliced
- 6 fresh basil leaves

Nutritional Information: 5 calories, 0g protein, 1g carbohydrates, 0g fat, 0g fiber, 0mg cholesterol, 0mg sodium

Directions:
1. Add cucumber slices and basil leaves to a pitcher of water.
2. Let infuse for 15 minutes before serving chilled.

4. Fresh Tomato Salsa

Yield: 4 servings   **Prep Time:** 10 minutes   **Cook Time:** 0 minutes   **Cooking Method:** No-cook

Ingredients:
- 4 medium tomatoes, diced
- 1/4 cup diced red onion
- 2 tbsp chopped cilantro
- 1 tbsp lime juice
- 1 clove garlic, minced

Nutritional Information: 30 calories, 1g protein, 6g carbohydrates, 0g fat, 2g fiber, 0mg cholesterol, 10mg sodium

Directions:
1. Combine all ingredients in a bowl. Stir gently to mix.
2. Serve immediately with whole-grain crackers or vegetable sticks.

5. Tzatziki Sauce

Yield: 4 servings   **Prep Time:** 10 minutes   **Cook Time:** 0 minutes   **Cooking Method:** Mixing

Ingredients:

- 1 cup plain Greek yogurt
- 1/2 cucumber, grated
- 1 clove garlic, minced
- 1 tbsp lemon juice
- 1 tbsp fresh dill, chopped

Nutritional Information: 50 calories, 4g protein, 3g carbohydrates, 2g fat, 0g fiber, 5mg cholesterol, 10mg sodium

Directions:

1. Combine all ingredients in a bowl. Mix well.
2. Chill for 10 minutes before serving with vegetables or grilled meats.

6. Rosemary and Lemon Olive Oil Dip

Yield: 6 servings   **Prep Time:** 5 minutes   **Cook Time:** 0 minutes   **Cooking Method:** Mixing

Ingredients:

- 1/4 cup extra virgin olive oil
- 1 tsp fresh rosemary, chopped
- 1/2 tsp lemon zest
- Pinch of sea salt

Nutritional Information: 80 calories, 0g protein, 0g carbohydrates, 9g fat, 0g fiber, 0mg cholesterol, 5mg sodium

Directions:

1. Combine all ingredients in a small bowl.
2. Serve as a dip for whole-grain bread or vegetable sticks.

7. Pomegranate Iced Tea

Yield: 4 servings   **Prep Time:** 5 minutes   **Cook Time:** 5 minutes   **Cooking Method:** Steeping

Ingredients:

- 4 cups hot water
- 2 green tea bags
- 1/2 cup pomegranate juice
- Ice cubes

Nutritional Information: 40 calories, 0g protein, 10g carbohydrates, 0g fat, 0g fiber, 0mg cholesterol, 5mg sodium

Directions:

1. Steep tea bags in hot water for 5 minutes. Remove tea bags and let cool.
2. Stir in pomegranate juice and serve over ice.

8. Basil Pesto

Yield: 6 servings   **Prep Time:** 5 minutes   **Cook Time:** 0 minutes   **Cooking Method:** Blending

Ingredients:

- 2 cups fresh basil leaves
- 1/4 cup olive oil
- 2 tbsp grated Parmesan cheese
- 2 tbsp pine nuts
- 1 clove garlic

Nutritional Information: 90 calories, 2g protein, 1g carbohydrates, 9g fat, 0g fiber, 5mg cholesterol, 30mg sodium

Directions:

1. Blend all ingredients in a food processor until smooth.
2. Serve as a condiment or toss with pasta.

9. Classic Mediterranean Lemonade

Yield: 4 servings   **Prep Time:** 5 minutes   **Cook Time:** 0 minutes   **Cooking Method:** Mixing

Ingredients:

- 4 cups cold water
- 1/2 cup freshly squeezed lemon juice
- 2 tbsp honey or maple syrup
- Ice cubes

Nutritional Information: 40 calories, 0g protein, 11g carbohydrates, 0g fat, 0g fiber, 0mg cholesterol, 5mg sodium

Directions:

1. Combine water, lemon juice, and honey in a pitcher. Stir until honey is dissolved.
2. Serve over ice for a refreshing drink.

10. Garlic Aioli

Yield: 4 servings   **Prep Time:** 5 minutes   **Cook Time:** 0 minutes   **Cooking Method:** Mixing

Ingredients:

- 1/2 cup Greek yogurt
- 1 clove garlic, minced
- 1 tbsp olive oil
- 1/2 tsp lemon juice

Nutritional Information: 50 calories, 2g protein, 1g carbohydrates, 4g fat, 0g fiber, 2mg cholesterol, 10mg sodium

Directions:

1. Mix all ingredients in a bowl until smooth.
2. Serve as a condiment or dip for roasted vegetables or fish.

11. Spicy Red Pepper Hummus

Yield: 4 servings   **Prep Time:** 10 minutes   **Cook Time:** 0 minutes   **Cooking Method:** Blending

Ingredients:

- 1 can (15 oz) chickpeas, rinsed and drained
- 1 roasted red pepper
- 2 tbsp tahini
- 1 tbsp olive oil
- 1 clove garlic, minced

Nutritional Information: 110 calories, 4g protein, 12g carbohydrates, 5g fat, 3g fiber, 0mg cholesterol, 60mg sodium

Directions:

1. Blend all ingredients in a food processor until smooth.
2. Serve with pita bread or vegetable sticks.

12. Iced Herbal Tea with Mint

Yield: 4 servings   **Prep Time:** 5 minutes   **Cook Time:** 5 minutes   **Cooking Method:** Steeping

Ingredients:

- 4 cups hot water
- 2 herbal tea bags (e.g., chamomile or peppermint)
- 1/4 cup fresh mint leaves
- Ice cubes

Nutritional Information: 5 calories, 0g protein, 1g carbohydrates, 0g fat, 0g fiber, 0mg cholesterol, 0mg sodium

Directions:

1. Steep tea bags in hot water for 5 minutes. Remove tea bags and let cool.
2. Add mint leaves and serve over ice.

CHAPTER 11: MEAL PLANS AND TIPS FOR MEDITERRANEAN LIVING

Welcome to your journey toward better health, vibrant flavors, and mindful eating with the 30-Day Mediterranean Meal Plan! Rooted in centuries-old traditions from the sun-soaked regions of the Mediterranean, this diet is more than just a way of eating—it's a lifestyle. Celebrated for its delicious simplicity and impressive health benefits, the Mediterranean diet is a sustainable, heart-healthy approach to nourishment that emphasizes fresh, whole foods and a balanced way of life.

Over the next 30 days, you'll experience a variety of colorful meals filled with wholesome ingredients like seasonal vegetables, ripe fruits, whole grains, legumes, nuts, lean proteins, and heart-healthy fats, particularly olive oil. Each day is thoughtfully planned to provide a satisfying balance of nutrients without sacrificing flavor or convenience. Whether you're a seasoned foodie or new to the Mediterranean diet, this meal plan will help you discover the joys of eating well while supporting your overall well-being.

By the end of this month, you'll not only have enjoyed a wide array of meals but also cultivated habits and recipes that can become a lifelong foundation for healthier living. So, tie on your apron, stock up your pantry with Mediterranean essentials, and get ready to savor every bite!

30-Day Meal Plan and Shopping List
Breakfast, lunch, dinner, and snacks planned for a week.

WEEK 1 MEAL PLAN	
BREAKFAST	
Day 1	Smoked Salmon and Arugula Wrap (pg 15)
Day 2	Whole-Grain Porridge with Almond Butter (pg 14)
Day 3	Banana Oat Smoothie (pg 20)
Day 4	Warm Lentil and Spinach Breakfast Bowl (pg 20)
Day 5	Mediterranean Breakfast Bowl (pg 16)
Day 6	Spinach and Ricotta Frittata (pg 16)
Day 7	Avocado Toast with Cherry Tomatoes and Feta (pg 13)
SNACK	
Day 1	Spinach and Feta Phyllo Triangles (pg 49)
Day 2	Cucumber and Tomato Salad with Feta (pg 52)
Day 3	Spiced Lentil Patties (pg 48)
Day 4	Roasted Red Pepper Dip (Muhammara) (pg 48)
Day 5	Baked Falafel (pg 47)
Day 6	Classic Hummus (pg 5)
Day 7	Marinated Olives (pg 46)
LUNCH	
Day 1	Zucchini Noodle and Shrimp Bowl (pg 35)
Day 2	Chickpea and Spinach Stir-Fry (pg 30)
Day 3	Grilled Chicken and Vegetable Wraps (pg 29)
Day 4	Lemon Orzo with Asparagus (pg 31)
Day 5	Tomato and Feta Stuffed Peppers (pg 33)
Day 6	Caprese Stuffed Portobello Mushrooms (pg 30)
Day 7	Grilled Vegetable and Hummus Wrap (pg 32)
DINNER	
Day 1	Baked Cod with Cherry Tomatoes and Olives (pg 41)
Day 2	Grilled Swordfish with Olive Tapenade (pg 40)
Day 3	Zucchini and Tomato Pasta (pg 43)
Day 4	Lemon Herb Grilled Salmon (pg 38)
Day 5	Ratatouille with Chickpeas (pg 40)
Day 6	Chicken Souvlaki Skewers (pg 42)
Day 7	One-Pan Mediterranean Chicken and Vegetables (pg 39)

WEEK 1 SHOPPING LIST		
Ingredient	Quantity	Unit
Smoked Salmon	4	oz
Arugula	2	cups
Tortilla Wraps	8	pieces
Oats	1.5	cups
Almond Butter	0.5	tbsp
Honey	0.25	tbsp
Bananas	2	pieces
Milk	2	cups
Lentils	2	cups
Spinach	4	cups
Eggs	6	pieces
Tomatoes	8	pieces
Cucumber	2	2
Phyllo Dough	1	sheets
Feta Cheese	3	oz
Cumin	0.5	tsp
Onions	1	pieces
Red Peppers	2	pieces
Walnuts	0.5	cups
Olive Oil	0.25	tbsp
Chickpeas	3	units
Parsley	0.5	cups
Garlic	3	cloves
Zucchini	5	pieces
Shrimp	1	lbs
Chicken Breast	1	lbs
Bell Peppers	4	pieces
Orzo	1	cups
Asparagus	1	bunches
Lemons	2	pieces
Cod	1	lbs
Cherry Tomatoes	1	cups
Olives	0.5	cups
Swordfish	1	lbs
Olive Tapenade	0.5	units
Pasta	1	cups
Salmon	1	lbs
Herbs	0.25	tbsp
Eggplant	1	pieces

WEEK 2 MEAL PLAN	
BREAKFAST	
Day 8	Zucchini and Feta Breakfast Muffins (pg 15)
Day 9	Banana Oat Smoothie (pg 20)
Day 10	Whole-Wheat Pancakes with Honey and Berries (pg 18)
Day 11	Roasted Red Pepper and Goat Cheese Frittata (pg 19)
Day 12	Spinach and Ricotta Frittata (pg 16)
Day 13	Smoked Salmon and Arugula Wrap (pg 15)
Day 14	Greek Yogurt with Honey and Fresh Fruit (pg 13)
Day 15	Mediterranean Veggie Omelet (pg 14)

SNACK	
Day 8	Classic Hummus (pg 45)
Day 9	Mediterranean Zucchini Fritters (pg 49)
Day 10	Spiced Lentil Patties (pg 48)
Day 11	Stuffed Grape Leaves (Dolmas) (pg 46)
Day 12	Baked Falafel (pg 47)
Day 13	Tzatziki Dip (pg 45)
Day 14	Spinach and Feta Phyllo Triangles (pg 49)
Day 15	Baba Ganoush (pg 50)

LUNCH	
Day 8	Mediterranean Chicken Salad Bowl (pg 32)
Day 9	Shrimp and Avocado Salad (pg 31)
Day 10	Mediterranean Tuna Salad (pg 29)
Day 11	Mediterranean Egg Salad (pg 35)
Day 12	Lemon Orzo with Asparagus (pg 31)
Day 13	Roasted Cauliflower and Chickpea Bowl (pg 31)
Day 14	Grilled Halloumi and Vegetable Salad (pg 36)
Day 15	Mediterranean Chickpea Buddha Bowl (pg 33)

DINNER	
Day 8	Lemon Herb Grilled Salmon (pg 38)
Day 9	Ratatouille with Chickpeas (pg 40)
Day 10	Mediterranean Stuffed Bell Peppers (pg 38)
Day 11	Greek-Style Grilled Chicken with Tzatziki (pg 37)
Day 12	Eggplant and Lentil Stew (pg 44)
Day 13	Chicken Souvlaki Skewers (pg 42)
Day 14	Roasted Cauliflower Steak with Tahini Sauce (pg 43)
Day 15	Grilled Swordfish with Olive Tapenade (pg 40)

WEEK 2 SHOPPING LIST		
Ingredient	**Quantity**	**Unit**
Bananas	2	pieces
Oats	0.5	cups
Milk	2	cups
Smoked Salmon	4	oz
Arugula	2	cups
Tortilla Wraps	4	pieces
Lentils	1	cups
Cumin	0.5	tsp
Onions	1	pieces
Chickpeas	2	units
Parsley	0.5	cups
Garlic	1	cloves
Phyllo Dough	1	sheets
Spinach	2	cups
Feta Cheese	1	oz
Orzo	1	cups
Asparagus	1	bunches
Lemons	2	pieces
Salmon	1	lbs
Herbs	0.25	tbsp
Eggplant	1	pieces
Zucchini	1	pieces
Swordfish	1	lbs
Olive Tapenade	0.5	units

WEEK 3 MEAL PLAN	
BREAKFAST	
Day 16	Mediterranean Chickpea Toast (pg 19)
Day 17	Roasted Red Pepper and Goat Cheese Frittata (pg 19)
Day 18	Greek Yogurt with Honey and Fresh Fruit (pg 13)
Day 19	Mediterranean Veggie Omelet (pg 14)
Day 20	Tomato and Spinach Egg White Scramble (pg 17)
Day 21	Banana Oat Smoothie (pg 20)
Day 22	Caprese Avocado Toast (pg 18)
Day 23	Warm Lentil and Spinach Breakfast Bowl (pg 20)
SNACK	
Day 16	Baba Ganoush (pg 50)
Day 17	Spinach and Feta Phyllo Triangles (pg 49)
Day 18	Cucumber and Tomato Salad with Feta (pg 52)
Day 19	Tzatziki Dip (pg 45)
Day 20	Baked Falafel (pg 47)
Day 21	Roasted Red Pepper Dip (Muhammara) (pg 48)
Day 22	Grilled Vegetable Skewers (pg 51)
Day 23	Spicy Red Lentil Dip (pg 52)
LUNCH	
Day 16	Mediterranean Chicken Salad Bowl (pg 32)
Day 17	Grilled Chicken and Vegetable Wraps (pg 29)
Day 18	Grilled Salmon with Lemon and Dill (pg 34)
Day 19	Mediterranean Tuna Salad (pg 29)
Day 20	Zucchini Noodle and Shrimp Bowl (pg 35)
Day 21	Shrimp and Avocado Salad (pg 31)
Day 22	Caprese Stuffed Portobello Mushrooms (pg 30)
Day 23	Grilled Halloumi and Vegetable Salad (pg 36)

DINNER	
Day 16	Ratatouille with Chickpeas (pg 40)
Day 17	Spinach and Feta Stuffed Chicken Breasts (pg 42)
Day 18	Zucchini and Tomato Pasta (pg 43)
Day 19	Shrimp and Spinach Orzo (pg 39)
Day 20	Roasted Cauliflower Steak with Tahini Sauce (pg 43)
Day 21	Baked Cod with Cherry Tomatoes and Olives (pg 41)
Day 22	Baked Tilapia with Lemon and Garlic (pg 44)
Day 23	Stuffed Eggplant with Ground Turkey (pg 41)

WEEK 3 SHOPPING LIST		
Ingredient	**Quantity**	**Unit**
Bananas	2	pieces
Oats	0.5	cups
Milk	2	cups
Lentils	1	cups
Spinach	3	cups
Phyllo Dough	1	sheets
Feta Cheese	2	oz
Cucumber	1	pieces
Tomatoes	4	pieces
Chickpeas	2	units
Parsley	0.5	cups
Garlic	2	cloves
Red Peppers	2	pieces
Walnuts	0.5	cups
Olive Oil	0.25	tbsp
Chicken Breast	1	lbs
Tortilla Wraps	4	pieces
Bell Peppers	2	pieces
Zucchini	5	pieces
Shrimp	1	lbs
Eggplant	1	pieces
Pasta	1	cups
Cod	1	lbs
Cherry Tomatoes	1	cups
Olives	0.5	cups

WEEK 4 MEAL PLAN	
BREAKFAST	
Day 24	Mediterranean Breakfast Bowl (pg 16)
Day 25	Mediterranean Veggie Omelet (pg 14)
Day 26	Caprese Avocado Toast (pg 18)
Day 27	Zucchini and Feta Breakfast Muffins (pg 15)
Day 28	Avocado Toast with Cherry Tomatoes and Feta (pg 13)
Day 29	Smoked Salmon and Arugula Wrap (pg 15)
Day 30	Mediterranean Chickpea Toast (pg 19)
SNACK	
Day 24	Grilled Halloumi Skewers (pg 47)
Day 25	Baked Falafel (pg 47)
Day 26	Spinach and Feta Phyllo Triangles (pg 49)
Day 27	Tzatziki Dip (pg 45)
Day 28	Spicy Red Lentil Dip (pg 52)
Day 29	Marinated Olives (pg 46)
Day 30	Mediterranean Zucchini Fritters (pg 49)
LUNCH	
Day 24	Roasted Cauliflower and Chickpea Bowl (pg 36)
Day 25	Lemon Orzo with Asparagus (pg 31)
Day 26	Grilled Halloumi and Vegetable Salad (pg 36)
Day 27	Caprese Stuffed Portobello Mushrooms (pg 30)
Day 28	Mediterranean Chickpea Buddha Bowl (pg 33)
Day 29	Mediterranean Tuna Salad (pg 29)
Day 30	Grilled Vegetable and Hummus Wrap (pg 32)
DINNER	
Day 24	Spinach and Feta Stuffed Chicken Breasts (pg 42)
Day 25	Greek-Style Grilled Chicken with Tzatziki (pg 37)
Day 26	Baked Tilapia with Lemon and Garlic (pg 44)
Day 27	Stuffed Eggplant with Ground Turkey (pg 41)
Day 28	Zucchini and Tomato Pasta (pg 43)
Day 29	Lemon Herb Grilled Salmon (pg 38)
Day 30	Grilled Swordfish with Olive Tapenade (pg 40)

WEEK 4 SHOPPING LIST		
Ingredient	Quantity	Unit
Eggs	6	pieces
Tomatoes	4	pieces
Cucumber	1	pieces
Smoked Salmon	4	oz
Arugula	2	cups
Tortilla Wraps	4	pieces
Chickpeas	1	units
Parsley	0.5	cups
Garlic	1	cloves
Phyllo Dough	1	sheets
Spinach	2	cups
Feta Cheese	1	oz
Orzo	1	cups
Asparagus	1	bunches
Lemons	2	pieces
Zucchini	2	pieces
Pasta	1	cups
Salmon	1	lbs
Herbs	0.25	tbsp
Swordfish	1	lbs
Olive Tapenade	0.5	units

Congratulations on completing your 30-Day Mediterranean Meal Plan! Over the past month, you've embraced a lifestyle celebrated for its vibrant flavors, fresh ingredients, and numerous health benefits. By incorporating wholesome foods, heart-healthy fats, lean proteins, and nutrient-rich produce into your daily routine, you've taken meaningful steps toward improving your overall well-being.

This journey has been about more than just meals—it's been about cultivating habits that nourish your body, mind, and soul. You've discovered how easy and enjoyable it can be to prepare meals filled with Mediterranean-inspired flavors, whether for a busy weekday breakfast or a relaxing dinner with loved ones. Most importantly, you've experienced the joy of eating mindfully, savoring every bite, and appreciating the simple pleasures of wholesome food.

As you move forward, we encourage you to continue incorporating the principles of the Mediterranean diet into your life. Use this plan as a foundation to explore new recipes, experiment with seasonal ingredients, and create balanced meals that fit your personal preferences. Remember, the Mediterranean lifestyle is not about strict rules or deprivation—it's about balance, variety, and enjoying the journey.

By sustaining these habits, you'll not only maintain the physical benefits of this diet but also foster a deeper connection to the food you eat and the people you share it with. Here's to many more delicious, healthy, and fulfilling meals ahead. Cheers to your health and happiness! 🌿🌱

Tips for Mediterranean Living

Prioritize Fresh, Seasonal Ingredients

Whenever possible, choose fresh, locally-sourced produce. Seasonal fruits and vegetables not only taste better but are often more nutrient-dense and budget-friendly. Visit farmers' markets or try growing your own herbs and greens for an authentic Mediterranean touch.

Make Olive Oil Your Go-To Fat

Extra virgin olive oil is a cornerstone of the Mediterranean diet. Use it as your primary cooking oil, drizzle it over salads, or pair it with whole-grain bread for a quick snack. Rich in healthy monounsaturated fats and antioxidants, olive oil adds depth and flavor to every dish.

Embrace Whole Grains and Legumes

Swap refined grains for whole grains like quinoa, bulgur, farro, and whole-wheat pasta. Incorporate legumes such as lentils, chickpeas, and beans into your meals to add plant-based protein, fiber, and flavor.

Eat More Plant-Based Meals

While lean proteins like fish and poultry are integral to the Mediterranean diet, plant-based meals should take center stage. Incorporate dishes that highlight vegetables, grains, legumes, and nuts for a lighter, nutrient-packed option.

Enjoy Seafood at Least Twice a Week

Fresh fish like salmon, tuna, sardines, and cod are rich in omega-3 fatty acids, which promote heart and brain health. Aim to include seafood in your lunches or dinners a couple of times each week.

Moderate Dairy Consumption

Choose high-quality, minimally processed dairy products like Greek yogurt, feta cheese, or ricotta. These add creaminess and flavor to your meals while providing calcium and protein in moderation.

Flavor with Herbs and Spices
Enhance the natural taste of your dishes with Mediterranean staples like oregano, basil, thyme, rosemary, garlic, and lemon. These add incredible flavor without extra calories or sodium.

Practice Mindful Eating
Take your time to savor each bite, enjoy meals with family and friends, and practice portion control. The Mediterranean way of eating values quality over quantity and emphasizes the joy of sharing food with others.

Hydrate Wisely
Drink plenty of water throughout the day, and enjoy herbal teas like chamomile or mint. A glass of red wine can also be part of your meals, but keep it moderate—typically one glass per day for women and two for men.

Make Physical Activity Part of Your Routine
Complement your Mediterranean diet with regular physical activity. Walk, swim, bike, or practice yoga to keep your body active and your mind refreshed.

By following these tips and embracing the Mediterranean lifestyle, you'll not only improve your physical health but also enjoy a more balanced and fulfilling relationship with food. Here's to a flavorful and nourishing journey!

CONCLUSION
Celebrate the Joy of Mediterranean Eating

As we reach the end of this culinary journey through the Mediterranean, it's time to celebrate not just the recipes you've explored, but the joy, health, and vitality that this way of eating can bring to your life. The Mediterranean diet is so much more than a collection of meals—it's a way of living that embraces flavor, mindfulness, and connection.

With its vibrant, nutrient-packed dishes and a focus on simplicity, the Mediterranean lifestyle invites you to savor every bite, prioritize fresh ingredients, and share meals with loved ones. It's about celebrating food as a source of nourishment and pleasure, not a source of stress or restriction. It's about finding balance—not perfection—and making small, sustainable changes that bring lasting benefits to your health and happiness.

This cookbook is your guide to making Mediterranean eating a permanent part of your life. Whether you're preparing a quick breakfast, a satisfying lunch, or a feast for family and friends, you now have the tools and recipes to bring the flavors of the Mediterranean to your table every day.

Remember, this isn't just a diet—it's a lifestyle filled with opportunities to connect with others, enjoy wholesome foods, and embrace a healthier, more vibrant way of living. As you continue this journey, let these recipes inspire you to experiment, explore, and create meals that reflect your unique tastes and traditions.

Thank you for allowing this book to be part of your Mediterranean adventure. May it be the start of a lifelong love affair with this timeless, healthful, and delicious way of life. Here's to savoring every moment, every meal, and every bite. Cheers to your health, your joy, and your future filled with Mediterranean sunshine! 🌿🍽️🥂

KITCHEN MEASUREMENTS CONVERSION CHART

Dry Weights

⚖️ oz	🥄	☕	⚖️ g	⚖️ lb
1/2 OZ	1 tbsp	1/16 C	15 g	-
1 OZ	2 tbsp	1/8 C	28 g	-
2 OZ	4 tbsp	1/4 C	57 g	-
3 OZ	6 tbsp	1/3 C	85 g	-
4 OZ	8 tbsp	1/2 C	115 g	1/4 lb
8 OZ	16 tbsp	1 C	227 g	1/2 lb
12 OZ	24 tbsp	1 1/2 C	340 g	3/4 lb
16 OZ	32 tbsp	2 C	455 g	1 lb

Egg Timer

Soft: 5 min.

Medium: 7 min.

Hard: 9 min.

Oven Temperature

ºF	ºC
500	260
475	240
450	230
425	220
400	200
375	190
350	180
325	170
300	150
275	140
250	120
225	110

10
9
8
7
6
5
4
3
2
1
1/2
1/4

Liquid Conversion

1 Gallon
4 quarts
8 pints
16 cups
128 fl oz
3.8 liters

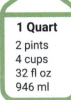

1 Quart
2 pints
4 cups
32 fl oz
946 ml

1 Cup
16 tbsp
8 fl oz
240 ml

1 Pint
2 cups
16 fl oz
470 ml

1/4 Cup
4 tbsp   2 fl oz
12 tsp   60 ml

Liquid Volumes

1 tsp = 5 ml

1 Tbsp = 15 ml

Dash = 1/8 tsp
Pinch = 1/16 tsp

⚖️ oz	🥄	🥄	🫗 ml	☕ C	pt	qt
1 OZ	6 tsp	2 tbsp	30 ml	1/8 C	-	-
2 OZ	12 tsp	4 tbsp	60 ml	1/4 C	-	-
2 2/3 OZ	16 tsp	5 tbsp	80 ml	1/3 C	-	-
4 OZ	24 tsp	8 tbsp	120 ml	1/2 C	-	-
5 1/3 OZ	32 tsp	11 tbsp	160 ml	2/3 C	-	-
6 OZ	36 tsp	12 tbsp	177 ml	3/4 C	-	-
8 OZ	48 tsp	16 tbsp	240 ml	1 C	1/2 pt	1/4 qt
16 OZ	96 tsp	32 tbsp	470 ml	2 C	1 pt	1/2 qt
32 OZ	192 tsp	64 tbsp	950 ml	4 C	2 pt	1 qt

INDEX

BONUS E-BOOK

YOU can get this ebook for free after sending me your name and email address.

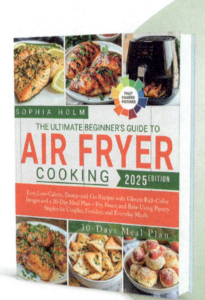

GET THIS E-BOOK FOR

FREE

YOU can get this ebook for free after sending me your name and email address.

kdpmasterinc@gmail.com